MONK HABITS
FOR
EVERYDAY
PEOPLE

Benedictine Spirituality
for *Protestants*

DENNIS OKHOLM

Brazos
Grand Rapids,

D0905761

Published by Brazos Press
a division of Baker Publishing Group
P.O. Box 6287, Grand Rapids, MI 49516-6287
www.brazospress.com

Printed in the United States of America

Library of Congress Cataloging-in-Publication Data
Okholm, Dennis L.
    Monk habits for everyday people : Benedictine spirituality for Protestants / Dennis Okholm.
        p.   cm.
    Includes bibliographical references.
    ISBN 10: 1-58743-185-8 (pbk.)
    ISBN 978-1-58743-185-2 (pbk.)
    1. Spirituality—Christianity. 2. Christian life. 3. Benedictines—Spiritual life. 4. Monastic and religious life. I. Title.
    BV4501.3.O456 2007
    255'.1—dc22   2007014959

To Sister Michaeleen Jantzer
who got me started
and
to Brother Benet Tvedten
who kept me going

CONTENTS

FOREWORD

During my first visit to a Benedictine monastery I was struck by what a good place it was to be as a Protestant. It wasn't only the extraordinary hospitality I encountered there—which I later learned is a core value of Benedictine spirituality—it was that I felt totally immersed in scripture. All day, every day, at morning, noon, and evening prayer, I was being asked to listen to the Bible, and let its words wash over me. At the Eucharist some words of interpretation were tossed in, but they were very few, as monastic homilies tend to be brief.

To hear entire psalms, and not just Sunday morning snippets, moving with the psalmist through the entire range of human emotion—from anger to joy, from bitter lament to exultant praise—taught me much about the nature of religious pilgrimage. To savor a minute of silence between each psalm, and two minutes after a scripture reading, allowed my heart to respond more fully. I was being shown a way to engage the Bible in a lively yet respectful manner such as I had never before experienced. It seemed that in just one day in the monastery I was hearing more scripture, and it was penetrating more deeply, than in a month of Sundays in the more hurried and "talky" worship of my Congregational, Methodist, and Presbyterian heritage.

My attraction to monastic liturgy did not mean that I was becoming a Catholic. Instead, it threatened to turn me into a better Protestant, one who was more attentive to the power of the Word. And this, I saw, was the fruit of genuine hospitality, which is not about turning others into people just like you but rather helping them to discover their own true selves. For someone who was just making her way back to church after many years, it was an unexpected and inestimable gift to be reintroduced to the Bible in such a powerful way.

I later learned that at around the same time, in a Benedictine abbey several hundred miles to the east, Dennis Okholm was having much the same experience. We were in fact part of a significant grassroots movement in American spirituality. Beginning in the 1960s, after Vatican II, many Protestants were discovering monasteries as places of spiritual renewal. Some were even becoming oblates (or associates) of these Christian communities. Today, in any Benedictine guest house, one will encounter laypeople and clergy from a wide range of denominations. There I have met Episcopalian, United Church of Christ, Church of the Nazarene, Assembly of God, AME, Baptist, Presbyterian, Methodist, Disciples of Christ, and Lutheran pilgrims.

Given this great diversity, the monastery choir and guest quarters become in effect ad-hoc ecumenical assemblies where Christians can enjoy what they have in common—the psalms, the gospels, and the Lord's Prayer—and not worry too much about what divides them. As a knowledgeable pastor and theologian, Dennis Okholm proves an excellent guide to this phenomenon, offering a fresh perspective on what attracts Protestants to monasteries. He demonstrates that it is not just another case of Americans shopping around for their spirituality, but a genuine reclaiming of the taproot of Christianity, a reconnecting with a religious tradition and way of life that predates all of the schisms in Christendom. His afterword, a reflection on the Protestant reformers and their original objections to monasticism, is particularly valuable.

This memoir, gentle in tone and often humorous, is nonetheless full of challenges to Protestant comfort zones. Okholm, for example, recommends that churches searching for a new pastor use as a template Benedict's Rule on the qualities desired in an abbot. He asserts that in a culture addicted to consumption and celebrity, exposure to Benedictine life and prayer can be a shocking plunge into the real world. He believes that monasteries, by demonstrating the religious significance of Christian community to an individualistic society, are a true witness in the world, for the sake of the world.

When I became an oblate in 1986, the Anglican writer Esther deWaal's *Seeking God* was the only book I could find that came close to addressing my situation. Now there are many books to help Protestants understand that Benedict's Rule is not just of use to monks, but also to churches, married couples, families, and individuals seeking to pray in a more contemplative manner. It is especially important that we now hear from Dennis Okholm, who reminds us that for all Christians, good spiritual habits are good for our spiritual health; that "scripture is the original rule"; and that Christ is the point of it all, our true beginning and our end.

Kathleen Norris
June 2007

ACKNOWLEDGMENTS

This book is, in part, the result of twenty years of influence by Benedictine monastics who have participated in my ongoing sanctification. Preeminently these have included Sister Michaelene Jantzer, O.S.B., and Brother Benet Tvedten, O.S.B. The monks of Blue Cloud Abbey who are referred to *en masse* and by name with great frequency in this book have been very significant in my journey. Many I have met along the way, such as Fr. Joel Rippinger, O.S.B., have also helped me to appreciate the serious academic study of Benedictine history and practice.

Some of the richest times I have had with Benedictine monastics took place at the semi-annual meetings of the board of the American Benedictine Academy during the four years that they tolerated my membership. (The board even helped set up a rendezvous with my wife outside of Tucson, Arizona, as we combined a meeting of the board with a meeting of a husband and wife who were only able to see each other once a month during a year of separation due to vocational commitments and inconvenient divine providence.) And the ABA's biannual gatherings, as well as two national meetings of oblate directors that I was privileged to attend, have increased my understanding of many dimensions of Benedictine history, thought, and life, about which I would otherwise be ignorant. Each time I have met with Benedictine monastics and oblates at these meetings I have come away richer, deeper, and blessed.

The initial draft of this book was encouragingly received by Rodney Clapp, but his editorial comments and his suggestions for improving the manuscript spurred me on to make the book more accessible and applicable to the everyday lives of nonmonastics. Subsequent readings by Benet and by the very competent editing of Ruth Goring have not only made wise suggestions and necessary corrections, but have saved me from making some embarrassing misstatements. It's been a joy to work with Rebecca Cooper at Brazos Press; it's been reassuring to know that even though she was once one of my students, it didn't prevent her from being a very capable and professional managing editor.

I would be remiss if I did not mention that over the years many students at Jamestown College, Wheaton College, and Azusa Pacific University have had to endure courses and lectures that were generated out of my interest in Benedictines, medieval monasticism, and monastic spirituality. A few Benedictine audiences and many church adult education classes and retreatants (which my spell checker wants to rewrite as "retreat ants," a hint that they may have been more attracted to the donuts than to the speaker) have not only listened with patience, but have responded with honesty and thoughtfulness in ways that have forced me to reconsider or strengthen the case I am making in recommending Benedictine spirituality to Protestants. Of the churches from whom I have benefited in this regard, I must especially mention First

Presbyterian Church of Glen Ellyn, Illinois, and St. Andrew's Presbyterian Church of Newport Beach, California.

There are times when I have my doubts, but I am fairly certain that my wife, Trevecca, is glad that I only became a Benedictine oblate and not a full-fledged monk. In fact, she has very graciously supported and encouraged my involvement with monastics, and she shares with me the friendship of several professed Benedictines. Without the blessing of my partner in kingdom work, I would not have pursued what is represented in this book.

There are countless others I am sure I should acknowledge here, including many of those named and unnamed in the pages that follow. I ask their forgiveness for my oversights, but I trust they will be encouraged by the reason that the Apostle Paul gives for remaining steadfast and excelling in the Lord's work as he concludes his "resurrection chapter" in 1 Corinthians: "because you know that in the Lord your labor is not in vain" (1 Cor 15:58 NRSV).

Holy Saturday, 2007

Experience confirms that humility is a very slow business if it is authentic. A realistic estimate of the time needed to get to the summit would be forty or fifty years. This is partly because progress is rarely unqualified. In most people's lives, there are periods of backsliding, false starts are made, blind alleys entered. . . . Even if we do not suffer wastage of effort, much time is needed for the restoration of God's image in us. Anyone who zooms up the ladder without pause or hindrance is probably going to die young. For the rest of us, it will be a lifelong journey.—Michael Casey, *A Guide to Living the Truth*

Therefore, in a word, I interpret repentance as regeneration, whose sole end is to restore in us the image of God that had been disfigured and all but obliterated through Adam's transgression. . . . And indeed, this restoration does not take place in one moment or one day or one year; but through continual and sometimes even slow advances God wipes out in his elect the corruptions of the flesh, cleanses them of guilt, consecrates them to himself as temples renewing all their minds to true purity that they may practice repentance throughout their lives and know that this warfare will end only at death. . . . The closer any man comes to the likeness of God, the more the image of God shines in him.
—John Calvin, *Institutes of the Christian Religion* 3.3.9

Do not aspire to be called holy before you really are, but first be holy that you may more truly be called so.
—*Rule of Benedict* 4.62

What's a Good (Protestant Evangelical) Boy Doin' in a Monastery?

The crash awoke us at 5:00 a.m. in our Wheaton townhouse. My first thought was "Not even the monks are up *this* early!" It turned out my wife's eighty-year-old aunt had awakened long before the rest of us and, in her legally blind condition, bumped into a large wooden painting that hung above the landing on our staircase. She sent it crashing to the floor but kept on course as she felt her way along the wall.

She was fine and as cheerful as ever. But I was stunned. In just three short years from the time I first encountered a Benedictine monastery, my life had been so altered that my first waking thoughts were about monks. And on those usual occasions when a relative was not stumbling through our townhouse, my first morning words were "Open my lips, O Lord, and my mouth shall declare your praise" (Ps.

51:16). To paraphrase the 1960s Christian rock artist Larry Norman, "What's a good Protestant boy—reared as a Pentecostal and Baptist and taught to be suspicious of Roman Catholics—doin' in a monastic frame of mind?"

The answer has to do with a providential array of circumstances. The sequence begins in the fall of 1985, early in the fourth year of my first teaching position—a tenure-track post at Western Kentucky University. As a result of academic politics, our department hired a new chair whose degree was from one of the few remaining bastions of Enlightenment modernism. (This will put in context his announcement.) He wanted to meet each of us individually over lunch. Mine was one of the last appointments, and we were having a delightful conversation until, about an hour into our meal, he informed me that my doctorate in theology from Princeton Theological Seminary was not appropriate at a public university and that I would no longer be teaching at the university after the academic year was over.

Needless to say, I stumbled home in shell shock that afternoon, and our lives were immediately disoriented. We eventually rallied and trusted God to lead. But this was an occasion when one did not want to be reminded that a thousand human years equals one God year. God was very slow to give signals. As the end of the academic year and my paychecks came within sight, the search for a new position was not yielding results. In a perpetual state of angst, that year I worked to complete my dissertation while teaching full time, preached at two churches, oversaw a youth group program, took ordination exams, and joined my wife in the financial responsibility for our two preschoolers and my cancer-stricken mother-in-law, who lived with us in a recently purchased house. A ministerial colleague in our Presbyterian church took a stress test for me (apparently he didn't want to burden me with one more task) and told me I was "off the chart."

By God's grace and strength we never succumbed to our record-breaking achievement, but as we spent humid Kentucky evenings on our porch swing sipping daiquiris after the kids were in bed and mulling over our lack of options, little did we know that by the end of June our course would be set for North Dakota, where I would wear the hats of philosophy professor and chaplain at Jamestown College.

It came as a surprise to us because in our deliberations we had made two lists of states—those where we preferred to reside and those where we did not—and North Dakota was on neither list. But a phone call had come months after I had submitted my application to Jamestown and hours before I was to call a church in Lexington responding to its offer of a pastorate: the college wanted us to visit—immediately. After protests that focused on climatic conditions and geographical location, and after a trip that left us feeling that we had gone through a time warp, my wife, Trevecca, and I sat down before our dinner with the dean after a day of interviews at the college and felt peace overwhelm us: amazingly, this is where God wanted us.

Moving and establishing a new home, followed by eighteen months of hitting the ground running with ecclesiastical and academic responsibilities, left me desperately needing a retreat. Since our student body included many Roman Catholics (though it was a Presbyterian college, it was located in "Lake Wobegon"—the land of Lutherans and Catholics), a delightful Benedictine sister named Michaelene Jantzer had been assigned to the local parish primarily to minister to our Catholic students. This sincere, jovial, and wise woman, who would soon celebrate fifty years in the order, quickly became a dear friend. And since she was a native to the frozen tundra, I asked her advice for a place of retreat. Her response was the most unusual advice this Pentescostal-born, Baptist-bred, Presbyterian Protestant had ever heard: "Call Blue Cloud Abbey, a Benedictine monastery in South Dakota, ask to speak to the guestmaster, and request accommodations for a retreat."

Years before, we had given a formerly cloistered nun a ride to a Bread for the World meeting while at Trinity Evangelical Divinity School in Illinois. And two classmates in doctoral studies at Princeton had been nuns. And there had been a monastery near us in Bowling Green, Kentucky, where we had had a man with the title Prior as a guest at our dinner table one Easter. (Why he was on the guest list I don't remember.) But given that in these three encounters monks had entered into *my* world, I still knew virtually nothing about what I considered to be a relic of the Middle Ages. I certainly had never darkened the door of a monastery, let alone a Roman Catholic haven. Michaelene might as well have been recommending a completely foreign country, especially since this was several years before Kathleen Norris's first book *Dakota* and the best-selling CD *Chant* would reintroduce contemporaries to a group of celibates who were off most folks' radar screen.

So I started out on March 11, 1987, heading straight south for almost two hours before turning left and heading straight east for another two hours. (Traveling on Dakota highways doesn't require making too many turns.) As I drove up the steep driveway to the monastery, I had second thoughts. Fortunately, it was too cold and too far from home for me to contemplate turning around. I would stay the two nights and two days, joining the monks in four times of prayer each day, eating with them in their refectory, and carrying on long conversations about their experiences and the monastic way of life. (My nervousness was exposed one night during dinner: it was evident that I had become a source of amusement for two other guests at the table, and finally I figured out why. I was eating a piece of shortbread as if it were a dry biscuit, not realizing that it was meant to be the foundation for strawberries and whipped cream that I had missed on the buffet table. It had never occurred to me that monks might indulge in strawberry shortcake.)

When I left I knew I had experienced something profound and I would have to visit again. On the way home, when I made a stop at the Fargo mall for a pair of tennis shoes, I found myself feeling out of place in the consumer culture that had shaped me. No forty-eight-hour experience had ever left such a huge crater in my life.

In fact, I returned to the monastery a few months later to plan a ten-day January-term class on monasticism, titled "The Habits of Monks." Six Protestant college students joined me for the class, entering the strange new world that I had encountered a winter earlier. It changed some of their lives, and it led me further down the path to become an oblate of Blue Cloud the following year, a participant in the biannual American Benedictine Academy meetings a year later, and the first nonmonastic (and non-Catholic) board member of the academy a few years after that.[1] In the meantime Benedictine monasticism has become the object of a good share of my academic studies, some of my course teaching, and a bit of my speaking and writing. But, even more, its spirituality has enriched my Christian life so much so that, as I tell my Benedictine friends, I am glad to be their evangelist to my Protestant brothers and sisters.

That's the reason for this book. Though there have been a growing number of books on Benedictine spirituality for the layperson since the 1984 publication of Esther deWaal's

Seeking God, only a few books have aimed specifically at sharing the wealth with Protestants *by* Protestants, particularly of the evangelical persuasion. Some of that is understandable, as I will elucidate. But I have read, seen, and heard too much to continue doling it out in bits of articles and speaking engagements. With some spice from a few sources outside Benedictine circles, I hope to entice Protestant readers (especially those like me whose pedigree includes Baptist and conservative evangelical strains), and others who care to join the circle, to include a helping of Benedictine tofu on their spiritual platter. My daughter, a vegetarian, tells me that tofu, when properly prepared, takes on the flavor of foods with which it is cooked. I hope that Protestants will find the Benedictine tradition similarly compatible with the savory portions that already occupy their spiritual plate. At the least it is healthier than much of the spiritual junk food that permeates our culture and satiates the appetites of folks who would do better to graze on something more nutritious.

In sharing the wealth, then, this book will hopefully serve as an *apologia* to my Protestant brothers and sisters who often understandably have misconceptions about monasticism, as well as objections to Roman Catholicism more generally. And the misunderstanding is not confined to the person in the pew. A prominent university professor and Protestant author of books on spirituality from which I have benefited gave an address at Wheaton College one year; afterward, when I posed a question, he simply dismissed any positive contribution that could come from the monastic tradition. I knew better, and I chalked up his comment to a lack of sympathetic acquaintance with the tradition.

Though my primary agenda is to commend Benedictine spirituality to heirs of the Protestant Reformers, I fully realize why this speaker rejected my appeal, given the repudiation of monasticism by the magisterial Reformers (e.g., Luther and Zwingli) and given the "semi-Pelagian" (translate "semi-heretical") label affixed to John Cassian, whose theology undergirds Benedict's *Rule*.[2] And because I have experienced this rejection or suspicion of monastic spirituality from evangelical Protestants more than from mainliners, this *apologia* is aimed especially, though not exclusively, at the former.

My intention is not to glamorize or idealize Benedictine monastic spirituality. One of my students recently covered his ears when I began to list examples of how contemporary monks do not live up to the ideals of Benedict's *Rule*. But my monastic friends would be the first to admit they do not measure up. And because I lack their humility, I would be the *second* to admit that I live nowhere close to the insights I will sketch in this book. (My little monastery of a nuclear family will vouch for that!)

In fact, Benedictine spirituality is not glamorous. It is *extraordinarily ordinary*. A few years ago, shortly after Kathleen Norris's second bestseller appeared (*The Cloister Walk*), I asked a monk who was traveling with me what he thought of her writing. He commended it, with one caveat: "She makes our life sound so interesting, but it's so d—n tedious." Benedict surely would have applauded, for his conception of monastic life rejected the goal of forming spiritual gold medalists or religious superstars. With no pun intended, it is a life of habits that, in turn, develop virtues (character traits) and muscles of the soul. Indeed, it aims at developing a healthy *whole* person.

Protestants do not usually go for the habitual when it comes to spirituality. For some reason we grow up with the bias that spiritual practice is "real" only if it is spontaneous. Habits (whether garments worn or behaviors cultivated) and read prayers often strike us as a fake spirituality. That was the reaction of one of my students the first time she heard the monks read psalms in a monotone during our ten-day adventure at Blue Cloud. She later learned that the lack of inflection facilitated hearing the words that were coming from the surround-sound choir rather than focusing on how well one was articulating the psalm in a cacophony of individual performances.

It is strange that we take the advice of our dentist and floss regularly to maintain healthy gums or follow doctor's orders to exercise on schedule to enhance our physical well-being, while we often spurn the counsel of spiritual physicians and trainers to develop habits that will maintain and enhance our spiritual life. It's not a bad thing to wake up every morning reciting the Psalmist's words "Open my lips, O Lord" as if it were second nature, any more than it is a bad thing to go through a morning ritual of showering, shaving, and brushing teeth.

I suppose that is why it has taken me nearly two decades to write this book. If I had written it a decade ago, it would have been as presumptuous as writing a manual on preparing to run the Boston marathon the year after I ran my first and only marathon—in flat Chicago. Even now I hesitate. I'm a spiritual adolescent. But like the typical adolescent, I dare to charge ahead.

2

WHY BENEDICTINE SPIRITUALITY FOR PROTESTANTS?

Richard Foster has said, "The desperate need today is not for a greater number of intelligent people or gifted people, but for deep people."[1] In many respects we live shallow lives, easily entertained by celebrities, trivial pursuits, and consumer products. A deeply rooted spiritual life is desired by many, but its cultivation seems to escape just as many. What does such a life look like? To what or to whom can we turn for guidance?

We are tempted to turn to the latest cleverly marketed book or to join the crowds that flock to hear a prominent Christian celebrity. We're modernists at heart: the latest is best and progress lies in going forward. But there are books and teachers that have proved effective by the long-term legacy they have left us, and they are worthy of rediscovery. Benedict is one of those.

What has been said of Aquinas could equally be said of Benedict: he was the "universal teacher of an undivided Christianity." When I first began to explore the roots of contemporary Benedictine monasticism, it dawned on me that in one sense Benedict belongs to Roman Catholics no more than he does to Protestants. His life preceded the Reformation by a millennium, and the same Protestants who revere and learn from Augustine (b. 354) may just as legitimately, and without feelings of betrayal and guilt, appeal to Benedict (b. 480).

Protestants share the same roots of Western Christianity with their unlikely Roman Catholic bedfellows, and this includes monasticism in its early and medieval stages. Though the movement had already begun, monasticism owes some of its early surge to the conversion of the fourth-century emperor Constantine and his subsequent endorsement of what became the "politically correct" Christian religion. When the state turned from persecutor to protector of Christianity, the church became "worldly" and the faith became secularized. Prosperity, patronage, doctrinal and political strife, and mixed motives for converting to Christianity and holding church office infected the church like viruses. In this setting monasticism became a reform movement—"a living protest against the secularization of Christianity and the cheapening of grace."[2] The protest took the form of withdrawal (*anchoresis* in Greek, from which we derive the word *anchorite*, meaning one who lives in seclusion) to the desert (*eremos*, from which we get the word *hermit*), literally following Jesus into the wilderness to fight the demons (Mark 1:13) and to achieve the perfection to which Christ called his disciples and which some thought to be unobtainable in

24

the existing churches and in contact with the world. With withdrawal came spiritual discipline (*askesis*, from which we get the word *ascetic* and which was applied to the rigorous training undertaken by those preparing for athletic and military contests).

Not all early monks spent their days alone. Many huddled in loose associations called *lavra*, while others formed communities (*cenobium*, a word combining the Greek *koinos* [common] and *bios* [life]) like the abbeys with which we usually associate monasticism today. Seeing the community as the sphere in which the Spirit worked, they lived under a common roof with a common authority, sharing possessions in a conscious attempt to imitate the communal life of the early church as described in Acts 2:42 and 4:32–36. Members of the community took vows of poverty, chastity, and obedience. These came to be known as the "evangelical" vows or "counsels of perfection." When he was about fifty years old, Benedict established such a community at Monte Cassino, located about sixty miles south of Rome. Here he spent the rest of his life, wrote his *Rule* for this specific monastic community, and gained a reputation as a holy man invested with divine gifts.[3]

But he was heir to the deteriorating political environment of the Roman Empire's last days. The fifth century into which he had been born had in common with our twenty-first a struggle to make sense of the troubled and torn world that people were experiencing. Rome had fallen and had been sacked several times, by the Goths, Vandals, and Lombards. The dismembered Western empire, once ruled by the "eternal city," was not only in political chaos but troubled by ecclesiastical dirty dealings and underhanded ploys to win theological battles over the crucial issues of grace and the divine nature of Christ.

It was to this kind of world that monasticism was responding with its regulated, disciplined, organized community life. Centuries later, the monastic movement that Benedict founded would be among the powerful forces working toward the civil and religious regeneration of the West. Most impressively, Benedictine monasteries preserved ancient literature that helped to make possible the cultural and religious achievements of the thirteenth century and the Renaissance of the fifteenth. But such achievements were byproducts of a deep interior life, cultivated by the legacy of a man who was intent on seeking God and who taught his followers how it should be done. By taking a critical stance toward the prevailing ethos, Benedict began a movement toward redemption of the created world whose fall Augustine had so eloquently described a century before in *The City of God*.

What guided his monks was the *Rule*, a practical guide for living the Christian gospel and for cultivating Christian virtue. It is less like the Law and more like the wisdom literature of the Old Testament (such as the book of Proverbs). It passed on a tradition of wisdom from the lived experience of monastic life. "With the Gospel for our guide" (*RB* prologue 21), the *Rule* did not so much dictate how to live as operate as a kind of flexible hermeneutical device to translate the gospel into daily communal Christian living. In a sense, it is not unlike the vows that pastors, elders, and deacons take in my denomination (Presbyterian Church USA) when we acknowledge that the confessions of our church are "authentic and reliable expositions of what Scripture leads us to believe and do" and promise to be "instructed and led by these confessions" as we lead God's people. Just as Presbyterian leaders have no intention of setting up any way of life other than the way of the gospel but seek guidance from the lived experience of those in our tradition as to how to live that life, so Benedict's *Rule* (*regula*) became the indispensable aid to help monks live according to scripture.[4]

The *Rule of Benedict* is about the size of the gospel account of Matthew, an average size given the fact that rules could range from a few hundred words to fifty thousand words. Benedict's *Rule* combines theoretical spiritual teaching in the first seven chapters (such as his description of humility) with practical regulations to govern the daily life of the monastery in the remaining sixty-six chapters. These deal with the time and quantities of food, sleep, and prayer, relations with the outside world, authority structures, and so on.

But again, scripture is the original rule. As the *Rule* states, "What page, what passage of the Old and New Testaments is not the truest of guides for human life?" (*RB* 73.3). Only twelve of the seventy-three chapters have no biblical allusions, and Benedict laced the entire *Rule* with quotes from the Bible—quotations that no doubt came from a memory that had been trained by countless readings in private and in community. Benedict's *Rule* reflects an interpretation of scripture that was applied to his single community, which he describes in the prologue as "a school for the Lord's service"—a community in which one could learn the trade or skill of discipleship as a Christian apprentice who desires to seek, know, and love God.

Though it was meant only for the monks at Monte Cassino, the *Rule of Benedict* became the most influential document in the entire history of Western monasticism. In fact, beginning with a decree of Charlemagne, it became *the* rule for Western monasticism from about 800 to 1200 (the "Benedictine centuries"), and it was copied more than any other piece of literature in the Middle Ages except the Bible. It was influential not because it was original—it wasn't! It borrowed heavily from an earlier and much longer but less adaptable rule, *The Rule of the Master*. It commanded such esteem because it was *traditional*—a masterful summary or synthesis of the whole preceding monastic experience. It didn't hurt that it was also brief, human, thorough, and adaptable. There is even some humor sprinkled here and there, such as in chapter 40, "The Proper Amount of Drink." Benedict writes, "We read that monks should not drink wine at all, but since the monks of our day cannot be convinced of this, let us at least agree to drink moderately, and not to the point of excess" (*RB* 40.6). From the quantity of wine to the steps to humility, Benedict's *Rule* translated the gospel into daily life with balance and realism.

To nonmonastic ears (and even at times to *monastic* ears), parts of Benedict's *Rule* may sound bizarre or extreme. For example, even though some of the best jokes I know came from monks, Benedict insists that monks are to avoid all "talk leading to laughter" (*RB* 6.8). And they are to "sleep clothed, and girded with belts or cords; but they should remove their knives, lest they accidentally cut themselves in their sleep." And "younger brothers should not have their beds next to each other, but interspersed among those of the seniors" (*RB* 22.5, 7). Modern readers are forewarned. Yet if we are charitable readers, our reactions to these directions may move us to question our biases and see things from another perspective. In an essay to incoming students at Wellesley College, Timothy Peltason warns, "Don't make the mistake either of thinking that when a book or a subject fails to please you that it's the book or the subject that's been found wanting."[5] We may blame the book for our inability to receive it, but reading an ancient text is like having a conversation with a person from another culture, and in the case of twenty-first-century Protestants, another faith community as well.

That's why Michael Casey suggests a "very active reading" of Benedict's *Rule*.[6]

So why might Protestants benefit from an examination of Benedict's rule and the spirituality it engendered? There are several reasons.

First, as Mark Noll has pointed out, to their credit Protestants, especially of the evangelical persuasion, have tended to be activist in their piety.[7] But, Noll argues, this has not always benefited evangelicals; they have sometimes neglected the development of the mind. And, we might add, they have similarly neglected the more contemplative side of the spiritual life. Further, evangelicals' activist piety tends to be individualistic. Minimally, the Benedictine tradition provides time and place for withdrawal from activity—for retreat and contemplation to balance what Catholics refer to as the "apostolic life" (the term Catholic monks use for the equivalent of what Protestants call pastoral or missionary work).[8] Moreover, the stress on community mitigates an unhealthy (and unchristian) individualism. Spiritual maturity develops not so much in one's closet as in the community's cloister. The Anabaptist tradition within Protestantism has been a notable exception to individualistic tendencies, and perhaps it should come as no surprise to learn that one of the early Anabaptist leaders, Michael Sattler, had been a Benedictine prior—an abbot's right-hand man. (By the way, there have been many notable Benedictines throughout history, such as Anselm of "the ontological argument for God's existence" fame and Thomas Merton.)

Second, a healthy ecclesiology demands that Protestants learn from their Benedictine brothers and sisters. In Ephesians 3:14–21 Paul prays that his readers will come to know the dimensions of God's reality "with *all* the saints." This was emphasized at my ordination, as I was charged with appreciating the various traditions out of which I had come (Pentecostal and Baptist) along with the one into which I had entered (Presbyterian). Little did I know at that time that this would eventually also include Roman Catholic Benedictines. But it makes sense given the strong emphasis on eschatology (the study of "last things") in evangelicalism: one day we will gather at the eschatological banquet, surrounded not only by God's chosen from every nation but also by his chosen from every branch of Christianity. Most likely, the Protestant who wrote off Roman Catholic Benedictine monastics will find that the Host of the banquet has placed him in a seat just to the right of this newly discovered brother, while just to the left may be the Eastern Orthodox sister he had rejected. Like little children in high society who take classes from Miss Manners so that they will be ready to conduct themselves appropriately at formal dinners, we Christians might as well practice rubbing shoulders with those who will share the table at the great banquet feast of the Lamb.

Third, Protestants have been very adept at formulating doctrine. It's hard to beat seventeenth-century Protestant scholasticism on this score. With logical precision we can outdo others in systematically wiring together an airtight theological system. The problem is that we are not always as good at *performing* our doctrines. Calvin said it well when he reminded us that doctrine is not merely a matter of the intellect or memory. Unlike disciplines such as mathematics, he insisted, doctrine is learned only when it resides in the heart and passes into our conduct, transforming us into itself in the process.[9] This is precisely the thrust of Benedictine spirituality: to appropriate truths of scripture and live them out in community. Hence the rationale for the rule.

Fourth, Protestants rightly place stress on scripture as the ultimate authority in matters of faith and practice. It is, to borrow a phrase used by Stanley Grenz, the "norming norm."[10] So we might be suspicious of Roman Catholic Benedictines' commitment to the authority of the magisterium (the authorized teachers of the Church's dogma). But we need to remember that Benedict came before not only the Protestant–Roman Catholic split but also the ascendancy of Rome's bishop to primacy in the West (a rise that was enabled, in part, by the incredible work of Rome's sixth-century bishop and arguably first significant pope, Gregory the Great—a churchman who is featured on one of the nine different tapestries in the "rotunda of witnesses" in Wheaton College's Billy Graham Museum, dedicated to the history of North American revivalism). More to the point, recent English translations of Benedict's *Rule* (such as *RB1980*,[11] the translation used in this volume) italicize quotations taken from the Bible. A cursory glance at the text makes it clear that nearly every other line includes an excerpt from scripture. One would expect this from a rule that was meant to apply scripture to daily living, composed by a man who was so steeped in the biblical text that it was no doubt part of his everyday speech.

Fifth, if nothing else, Protestants would do well to explore Benedictine monasticism to clear up some common misconceptions. For instance, often when I am teaching a college class on monasticism or lecturing at a church on my Benedictine experiences and lessons learned, I hear the complaint that I'm not talking about the "real world." Of course this begs the question. We must first determine what the *real* world is.

I learned something about this from one of my college students. As a high schooler, she had come back from a week at a Christian camp and told her father that she knew it was time to come down from the mountaintop and enter back into the real world. Her wise father answered her, "You *were* in the real world!" That is, the mountaintop experience of Christian community that she had experienced at camp more closely approximated the world as God intended it when he created the cosmos. What we have made of the creation (the "world" into which she reentered after camp) is not the way it was meant to be.

In fact, most of us in the marketplace live on the surface of life; like skipping stones that skim the top membrane of a lake, we make superficial contacts without really knowing the true depth of life above which we're gliding. The *real* world often goes undetected, hidden under the cloak of the culture's prevailing ethos.

So to those who say that the monastery is not the "real world," one might respond that the Benedictine life actually takes us far deeper into the real world than most other avenues of experience. It certainly is more significant than unreflectively flipping hamburgers at McDonald's eight hours a day and asking customers if they "want fries with that." At least that was my response to a college student who, after visiting a monastery, reported that he just did not see the point of spending all one's time in a praying community; I suggested he compare that to many of the activities we engage in day after day, for example the four hours and thirty-five minutes that the average individual in the United States spends watching television each day.[12] Is the monastic balanced life, which puts possessions and relationships and the life of the soul in proper perspective, less real than our consumptive preoccupation with gadgets, television, celebrities, war, and spirit-numbing work? Who has distorted reality: the monk or the materialist?

Though applied to another context (Holy Week), Richard John Neuhaus's words capture the disorientation I felt when

I visited the mall on my way home after my first retreat at a monastery:

> We contemplate for a time the meaning of Good Friday, and then return to what is called the real world of work and shopping and commuter trains and homes. As we come out of a movie theater and shake our heads to clear our minds of another world where we lived for a time in suspended disbelief, as we reorient ourselves to reality, so we leave our contemplation—we leave the church building, we close the book—where for a time another reality seemed possible, believable, even real. But, we tell ourselves, the real world is a world elsewhere. It is the world of deadlines to be met, of appointments to be kept, of taxes to be paid, of children to be educated. From here, from this moment at the cross, it is a distant country. "Father, forgive them, for they have forgotten the way home. They have misplaced the real world." Here, here at the cross, is the real world, here is the *axis mundi*.[13]

Finally, returning to Richard Foster's comment with which I began this chapter, in our desire to maximize our return on investments in reaching people for Christ, we Protestants of U.S. revivalist heritage are often captives of the consumer-driven, efficiency-minded, results-oriented culture in which we grow our churches. But Benedict and his contemporaries remind us that Christians mature more like trees than like fast-spreading computer viruses. (Consult the imagery in Psalm 1.) Indeed, the early monks practiced a way of life that we sometimes call *asceticism*. As mentioned earlier, it comes from the Greek *ascesis*, a word that was used in connection with the discipline an athlete engaged in to prepare for the Parthian or Olympic games. So *ascesis* is the training or exercise that a Christian *disciple* (or disciplined student of Christ) engages in, graciously empowered by the Spirit of God, in order to win the contests against sin and demons.

We know that exercise and proper diet are necessary if we are going to be physically fit, but we don't always realize that exercise and proper diet are necessary if we are going to be *spiritually* fit. We Protestants often seem to think that salvation consists only in forgiveness of sins and acceptance by God—the justification by grace through faith that the Reformers like Luther and Calvin rightly stressed. But that is not all there is to salvation. To use an image suggested by Dallas Willard in a talk he gave at Wheaton College years ago, evangelicals sometimes think salvation is like slapping a bar code on a person: once you've got the bar code of forgiveness and acceptance, you just wait around until the trumpet sounds, at which point you walk through the pearly gates as St. Peter scans you with his wand.

In the Protestant tradition, justification is only the God-initiated beginning—at our spiritual birth. We now have a whole lifetime of our salvation to work out, which the Bible and theologians call "sanctification." This is an aspect of our lives that has been emphasized especially by those in the Reformed and Holiness traditions of Protestant spirituality. But in recent years we have not always been good at stressing this. And it took the monks to help remind me.

When a person enters into a saving relationship with Jesus Christ, her soul is not fully developed, as Tom Hanks's body was overnight in the movie *Big*. You *begin* to be a student athlete of Christ, training yourself with spiritual exercises and a proper spiritual diet (and even a proper physical diet) so that you can develop muscles of the soul. (This is why annual Lenten discipline is important, by the way. To adapt one Benedictine monk's explanation, we engage in an annual spiritual checkup before Easter in order to locate the flab on our soul—the sin that is particularly ours; then we prescribe for ourselves a regimen of soul food and exercise to become more spiritually fit and gain a foretaste of the joy of heavenly existence.)

We often want the painless quick fix in our sanctification, like a guilt-free diet that demands no sacrifice or the PowerBar that will give us the carbs we need for the next half-hour's activity. We have become *consumers* of religion rather than *cultivators* of a spiritual life; we have spawned an entire industry of Christian kitsch and bookstores full of spiritual junk food that leaves us sated and flabby. As if we believed the infomercial that promises great abs if we just buy the right piece of equipment for $39.95, we think that the secret to being a spiritually fit Christian can be had by finding some secret technique or buying the most recent hot-selling inspirational devotional.

Maturity in the Christian life does not come in these ways. The life of the disciple is like that of the athlete who prepares for and runs a marathon. We can have the snazziest running garb, assemble a library full of training schedules and tips, and watch *Chariots of Fire* each day every day for a year, but while all of these things might help, they will not be a substitute for the unspectacular training and diet that we must engage in if we are going to become mature Christians, "perfect and complete, lacking in nothing" (Jas. 1:4). It's that way with anything in life—being a concert pianist, a skilled sculptor, or an insightful historian.

Of course, no pianist, sculptor, or historian would say she's finally "arrived." Neither would a Benedictine monk. In fact, Benedictines would probably be closer to Calvin's idea of never-ending progress in the Christian life this side of heaven than to Wesley's idea of "Christian perfection." Monks, like all Christians, are folks who participate in a shared life, forming and being formed into the likeness of Christ. It's a spiritual formation that involves the process of becoming perfect or complete (they're the same word in Greek) true human selves—something we lost and retain only the vestiges of after the fall. Just as Calvin spoke of the goal of sanctification, so the goal of Benedictine monastic life is the restoration in fallen humans of the divine likeness—the image of God.[14] In other words, Benedictine monasticism is just one way of being a disciple of Jesus Christ. Hopefully, then, this book will be an aid in the sanctification of Protestant individuals by offering bits of wisdom and strategies for growth gleaned from the Benedictine tradition.

In the end, the goal of the Protestant and the Benedictine is the same: to seek God. To the question "Do you seek God?" an affirmative answer is the only *essential* requirement for becoming a Benedictine novice. (Since Benedictine abbeys are sometimes as autonomous as Baptist churches, depending on house rules it may take up to nine years before a monk makes a final profession as a life-member of the community, though it is more usual for this to occur after the one-year novitiate and a minimal three-year period of "temporary vows.")

Several years ago I delivered the annual dean's convocation at an Anabaptist college in the Midwest at the request of my friend the dean. We dressed in full academic regalia so that when the fuzzy black-and-white photograph of me appeared in the local town newspaper I indeed looked like a monk dressed in his habit; and the photo fit the headline: "Monk Addresses College." I was a true monk for one day and didn't even realize it.

But I mention this incident because I ended a follow-up talk at the college with these words of Esther deWaal:

St. Benedict points to Christ. It is as simple as that. Christ is the beginning, the way and the end. The *Rule* continually points beyond itself to Christ himself, and in this it has allowed, and will continue to allow, men and women in every age to find in what it says depths and levels relevant to their needs and their understanding at any stage on their journey, provided that they are truly seeking God.[15]

The dean came up to me afterward and said, "That's *exactly* what I want." Indeed, that has always been a Protestant mantra—*sola Christi*.

What Benedictines have to offer Protestants in this quest is the lived reminder that the Christian community's ultimate function is to shape individuals who, as disciples of Christ, are being formed into his image. In fact, the test of any religious community that claims to be a *Christian* community is the extent to which the individuals in it, through their life together, are being transformed into the likeness of the one whose body they eat and whose blood they drink.

3

LEARNING TO LISTEN

The first words of Benedict's *Rule* are these: "Listen carefully, my son, to the master's instructions, and attend to them with the ear of your heart. This is advice from a father who loves you; welcome it, and faithfully put it into practice" (*RB* prologue 1).

Listening. It's not something for which Protestants are usually well known. In our activist piety we have tended toward prophetic pronouncements rather than quiet listening. As Father Guy, one of the first monks I met, put it, "Samuel said, 'Speak, Lord, for thy servant is listening'; we more often say, 'Listen, Lord, for thy servant is speaking.'"

Of course, listening requires a degree of silence—both within and without. We live in a noisy world. Wherever you are right now reading this, there is probably noise in your environment—from the hum of fluorescent lights to the sound of a ticking clock to a plane overhead or car outside.

Some friends of ours, who have lived in Orange County for many years, took a long-awaited trip to New Zealand. Afterward when I asked one of them what was memorable about the trip, his first reply was that it was so wonderfully quiet in the countryside. His experience was the converse of that of one of my students who spent ten days at Blue Cloud Abbey as part of my Habits of Monks course. After we had returned to campus, I asked each one what struck him or her about reentering the college environment. Brent responded, "I never knew how noisy the dorms were." The relative silence of the Benedictine abbey had made him even more aware of the sounds he had taken for granted. (And this wasn't even a Trappist monastery, such as the Cistercian abbey in Gethsemane, Kentucky, of which Thomas Merton was a member.[1] *That* is quiet!)

What Brent and the other students had experienced began with their entry into the lobby of the monastery during Vespers, as Brother Rene greeted us in hushed tones in a dimly lit foyer. The mood was set. It would continue after Compline (the last prayers of the evening before retiring) when the Great Silence begins—a silence that is broken by the first spoken words of the monk during Lauds (morning prayer) when all say in unison, "Open my lips, O Lord, and my mouth will declare your praise." The students also experienced the silent time of reflection after each psalm was recited and after the scripture lesson was read in the unhurried pace of the community's prayers. And all congregated for dinner in silence and ate without speaking while a designated reader regaled us with several pages from a book.

It is not that Benedict forbade his monks to speak. In his day there would have been little space and time that was private, since accommodations for everything from eating to sleeping were public. As a result, Benedict encouraged silence, especially during table reading in the refectory, at night in the dormitory, and in the oratory when monks were not engaged in communal prayer. When words were necessary, Benedict exhorted them, they should speak rarely, briefly, directly, and simply; speech that was malicious, gossip, tasteless, or destructive was forbidden. As Columba Stewart explains, "The issue becomes more clearly one of stewardship. Language is a gift that can be used thoughtfully or thoughtlessly, humbly or proudly. Someone constantly aware of the presence of God will know when and how to speak."[2]

Today the monks have more private space than in Benedict's day. At the same time, even *their* world is filled with noises generated by media, telephones, and electrical devices. Still, the modern abbey is as Brent experienced it—relatively quiet compared to the world outside the monastic enclosure.

We are always filling our world with noise. Even our Communion services must be filled with sound. Quietly reflecting on the fact that we are eating the Lord's body and drinking the Lord's blood seems too threatening; as soon as we go forward or pass around the elements, a piano or guitar starts up and we cannot even hear ourselves consume Christ.

Perhaps it's not just the silence itself that frightens us. Perhaps we fill our world with noise because we are really afraid to face ourselves. It was actually an Orthodox metropolitan, Anthony Bloom, who helped me to understand the threat of silence in our lives. In his book *Beginning to Pray* he writes,

> Settle down in your room at a moment when you have nothing else to do. Say "I am now with myself," and just sit with yourself. After an amazingly short time you will most likely feel bored. This teaches us one very useful thing. It gives us insight into the fact that if after ten minutes of being alone

with ourselves we feel like that, it is no wonder that others should feel equally bored! Why is this so? It is so because we have so little to offer to our own selves as food for thought, for emotion and for life. If you watch your life carefully you will discover quite soon that we hardly ever live from within outwards; instead we respond to incitement, to excitement. In other words, we live by reflection, by reaction. . . . We are completely empty, we do not act from within ourselves but accept as our life a life which is actually fed in from outside; we are used to things happening which compel us to do other things. How seldom can we live simply by means of the depth and the richness we assume that there is within ourselves.[3]

The noise distracts us, and we need not focus our attention on ourselves. In fact, if Bloom is correct, there is not much to attend to without outside stimulation. As Michael Casey put it, "There is no one at home in us except the flickering images we receive from outside."[4] I've often wondered what would happen if I were suddenly held hostage for several months, as were four members of the Christian Peacemaker Teams in Iraq in 2006. Would I have enough to offer myself as food for thought? I suspect that if for many years I had daily recited the Psalter, read scripture, and prayed at certain hours of the day, as a hostage I would not feel bored after ten minutes in a barren cell. It's a good thought experiment.

But the noise not only hides us from ourselves. It can also keep us from hearing and attending to the needs of others. Though it sounds trivial, I was surprised when at the end of my first retreat at a Benedictine monastery, Father Guy, the guestmaster, asked if I had a thermos. I had about a four-hour journey back home on a cold Dakota winter day. He was so attentive to my impending agenda that he thought I might enjoy hot coffee along the way. I hadn't asked for it, and my thermos was out of sight in the car, but apparently

Guy had discerned that if it had been *my* wedding at Cana I would have asked Jesus to change the water to strong black coffee. Guy had listened and heard a desire that I myself would not have become aware of until I was well on my way home along barren Dakota highways.

By learning to listen we can become attentive to God's action around us and to the needs of brothers and sisters— needs of which even they themselves are unaware. Just as the silence in Communion helps us to focus on the reality underlying our acts of eating and drinking, so learning to become aware of the sacramental presence of God in all of life is a feature of Benedictine spirituality that we might find very helpful in everyday life.

Life is not to be divided into airtight compartments, so that the activity of praying, for instance, has nothing to do with balancing our checkbook. God is somehow present in all of our activities—indeed, in all of reality, even the reality that is "described" by the entries in my checkbook. Stopping at points during the day to quietly engage in prayer (the Daily Office) or to be nourished by God in the Eucharist recenters and refocuses our attention on God's presence in all of life. Some contemporary Christian worship has a way of secularizing worship rather than sanctifying common life as the monastic office tends to do. More on punctuating the day with times of prayer will come in another chapter, but I think that the daily discipline of monastic prayer goes far to explain why Father Guy asked if I had a thermos.

The point is that Benedictine spirituality can help make us aware of God's presence in *every* area of life and in every encounter.[5] Neglecting this fundamental insight will leave our experience of God impoverished, for we will have closed off an aspect of life in which the omnipresent God could be known to us. A postcard I purchased in a Benedictine monastery's gift shop makes the point succinctly and quite well. I display it in my office as a reminder. It's a quote from Emily Dickinson: "Take care for God is here."

The disciplines of monastic spirituality refocus our attention on what is really going on around us, even when we *are* just flipping burgers. Monastic disciplines plunge us deeper into the reality of everyday life because we go deeper into God's reality. They plunge us beneath the surface of busyness to really notice the person who is next to us, to experience the joy of our children's pleasure at play, or to hear the seemingly endless variety of birds' songs.

Surely Protestants should resonate with the desire to appropriate the gospel in such a way that every moment of our life is lived in conscious awareness of the presence and activity of the God whom we profess to trust and love. But it is an awareness that must be shaped in us—formed in us—by good habits.

Anthony Bloom tells the story of cosmonaut Gagarin's return from space, when he made the remark that he never saw God in heaven. One of the priests in Moscow responded, "If you have not seen Him on earth, you will never see Him in Heaven." Bloom comments: "If we cannot find a contact with God under our own skin, as it were, in this very small world which I am, then the chances are very slight that even if I meet Him face to face, I will recognize Him."[6]

Before I end this chapter, there is an important aspect of listening we haven't discussed—*not talking*. It's an important and often misunderstood issue for Benedict that comes up early in his *Rule*, and we got a glimpse of it when we mentioned his prohibition against talking which leads to laughter.

Recently, on an Ash Wednesday, I was encouraging my students to think of one deficiency in their lives that they could attack with a spiritual discipline during Lent. Never afraid to barge in where uninvited, a member of the class in the back row (the source of much consternation for college professors) asked, "What deficiency are *you* going to attack?"

I had to be honest, so I answered, "Actually I've got several, and I need to decide on one by the beginning of the first full week of Lent. I'll let you know." But I knew what it would be, and, true to my word, I soon announced to the class that I needed to learn to listen better to others, so I would be attempting to talk much less in some small study groups of which I was a part.

What I attempted—with a mixed degree of success—was what Benedict insists upon all the time for his monks in chapters 6 and 7.56–61 of the *Rule*—namely, restraint of speech. He does not command silence (*silentium*) but restraint (*taciturnitas*), because sometimes silence can be a bad thing, such as when someone needs help with directions or counsel in a bad marriage or clarification to avoid misunderstanding. Benedict realized this might be the case, for instance, when guests are at the monastery (*RB* 42.10, 53.16). When a monk speaks, he should do so gently, seriously, briefly, and reasonably (7.60). What Benedict explicitly prohibits is talk that is obscene, slanderous, or empty (6.8).

Beside the advice from scripture that he cites (Ps. 39:1–2; Prov. 10:19, 18:21), why would Benedict be so concerned with a topic about which we hear so little in the church? Michael Casey answers with a litany of possible dangers of talk: "It restricts our capacity to listen, it banishes mindfulness and opens the door to distraction and escapism. Talking too much often convinces us of the correctness of our own conclusions and leads some into thinking they are wise. It can be a subtle exercise in arrogance and superiority. Often patterns of dependence, manipulation, and dominance are established and maintained by the medium of speech."[7]

Though we are all guilty from time to time of failing to restrain our speech when we should, a former colleague was a classic case of Benedict's concern. He had the habit of constantly interjecting a putdown, and though his hearty laugh made it clear to everyone that his comments were meant in jest, he was unaware of the cumulative effect this practice had on his relationships with friends and its reinforcement of a critical spirit in his life. Casey is correct when he warns that speech that is not subordinate to the Christian's fundamental purpose in life will "imperceptibly subvert our efforts," because many of our "daily sins" are launched by or performed in our conversation: often our spontaneous speech "sides with the part of us that resists grace."[8]

So if we want to grow in grace, we must learn to talk less and listen more. This will be inseparable from the practice of Benedictine poverty.

4

POVERTY

Sharing the Goods

Benedict discusses the ownership and distribution of possessions and goods in chapters 33 and 34 of his rule. He develops a working definition of *poverty* fashioned after the description of the New Testament church in Acts 4:32–25. Benedict's was not a Fransciscan concept of poverty—the *giving up* of all things. Instead, poverty is here understood as the *common ownership* of all things, something Benedict insists upon in the chapter describing the procedure for receiving brothers into the monastery (*RB* 58.24–26).

The idea is that all in the community must be free to share. It's akin to Martin Luther's notion that goods are not really "goods" unless they can be shared. Whatever the monk takes to his cell (and Benedictine monks today do "possess" their own clothes, alarm clocks, books, and other stuff) he is to take as a steward. In other words, the community should be the beneficiary even of that which the monk has as his "own."

Sister Michaelene, the monastic who encouraged my first foray to a Benedictine abbey, told me that when she was being "reared" in the community the nuns would inscribe their books with *ad usus* before their names—that is, "*for the use of* Sister Michaelene.*"* Perhaps that is an invisible stamp we should put on all of our possessions: a house, a car, a book, clothing . . . for the use of the steward of these goods.

This is a good corrective in a culture where greed and gain often put smart investments ahead of concerns for God's earth and other people. We live in a culture that consumes to the extent that avarice is no longer one of Gregory the Great's deadly sins but one of Donald Trump's virtues. (Gregory, a Benedictine, was actually the one who came up with our list of the seven "deadlies," after revising a list of eight that was passed on to him by Evagrius Ponticus and John Cassian, the theologian to whom Benedict commends us in the final chapter of his rule if we want to go further.)

For many conservative Protestants greed is not a virtue, but unfortunately it's simply not on the radar screen. Once when I was on a student life committee at a Christian college, I suggested that our students might be as addicted to consumption of material goods as they are to sex. I was rebuked by the dean of students, who asked me if I realized how many young people came to his office because they were troubled about sexual matters, while none came to him about problems with greed. I guessed that these statistics had more to do with the fact that sex, not avarice, was perennially discussed at our school (and in many of our students' home churches) than that the students had conquered the beast of greed. Ironically, one of my students who wrote a paper on greed admitted that he had run to the library to get books on the topic before other students beat him to it, but when he returned for bibliographical information about a monograph on greed that he had used, he discovered that someone had stolen it.

The Benedictine concept of poverty might also be a good corrective for Protestants who buy into a "work ethic" named after them. The Protestant work ethic is the notion that those whom God elects to be saved are those whose abundance is proof of privileged status: they are hardworking, frugal, and prosperous.

This notion rears its head in situations like the one my wife experienced shortly after we moved from North Dakota to the Chicago area. We could barely afford the condo we bought, given the much pricier locale and because we had recently sold our house in Kentucky at a significant loss after it had been on the market during most of the three years we lived in North Dakota. As my wife sat in a meeting at the college, a colleague's wife reported that they had just had their house appraised and it was worth much more than they had expected; *her* appraisal was that God had blessed them. When I heard this I wondered (facetiously) why God had skipped over the Okholms (and a few of my colleagues) with such blessings and whether folks like Donald Trump were also thanking God for blessing them with property and wealth.

Our assumptions tell on us. We often harbor the bias that poverty is a sign of sin when, without glamorizing it, it might be the result of being satisfied with little and wanting nothing. Benedict reminds us that the blessed life does not consist in the fulfillment of our material desires but in the redirection of all desires to our seeking of God and love of neighbor.

When a monk enters the monastery, he signs over all his worldly possessions to the monastery, or he gives them to family members or friends outside the monastery. The signing of a legal document is part of this ritual. This frees the monk to focus on greater things, since the lesser things are taken care of by the community as a whole. The monastery owns cars that can be "checked out" for use. A library in the cloister (the private monastic dorm, if you will) makes books, periodicals, and journals available to all. Even a pair of cross-country skis might be found in the monastery closet, as my students and I discovered when we sought a bit of recreation during our ten-day winter stay at the abbey. Food is prepared and shared from the common kitchen. And since the monk receives no private income, tax returns are not filed by individuals.

This can be quite freeing. For one thing, it frees a person to "hear" the needs of others and the voice of God, as discussed in the previous chapter. I recall the story (perhaps apocryphal) of a naturalist and his friend who were walking along a busy New York City sidewalk. The naturalist stopped abruptly and held back his friend. "Listen. Do you hear that cricket?" The companion was incredulous: "How can you hear a cricket with all this noise?" The naturalist replied, "We hear what we are trained to hear." Then he illustrated. He dropped a quarter on the sidewalk, and immediately a swarm of passersby stopped and looked.

We hear what we are trained to hear. And if we have been trained well to be possessive consumers, then we may not be well trained to hear the needs of others or the voice of God. In fact, we may actually lose the capacity to serve others.

Again, it's Orthodox churchman Anthony Bloom who nicely illustrates this feature of Benedictine spirituality. Encouraging his readers to be "free of being rich" and reminding us that we cannot store anything but treasures for the kingdom of God (as Jesus pointed out in Matthew 6), Bloom explains:

> The moment we try to be rich by keeping something safely in our hands, we are the losers, because as long as we have nothing in our hands, we can take, leave, do whatever we want.
>
> . . . Have you ever noticed that to be rich always means an impoverishment on another level? It is enough for you to say, "I have this watch, it is mine," and close your hand on it, to be in possession of a watch and to have lost a hand. And if you close your mind on your riches, if you close your heart so that you can keep what is in it safe, never to lose it, then it becomes as small as the thing on which you have closed yourself in.[1]

In chapter 34 of the *Rule*, Benedict makes an interesting concession. Based on the New Testament church's principle of distribution of goods according to need, Benedict says, "Whoever needs less should thank God and not be distressed, but whoever needs more should feel humble because of his weakness, not self-important because of the kindness shown him" (34.3–4). This reverses our culture's dogma that the powerful are those who possess more. Esther deWaal puts it poignantly: "The weak must have more things than the strong."[2] Some days I am very weak.

In his book *The Challenge of the Disciplined Life*, Richard Foster reflects on Paul's boast from his jail cell that he has learned to be content in all circumstances, including impoverishment and wealth.[3] Like most, I was impressed that Paul could be content in poverty, but insightfully Foster rightly points out that that is the wrong emphasis. For Paul, and for all of us, it is surely more difficult to be content when we have *more* things than when we have fewer. The more stuff we have the bigger locks we must install, and the more accessories we must buy, and the more time and energy we must consume to protect and care for what we have. (The proliferation of iPod accessories is proof enough.) Greed cannot cohabitate with contentment.

Indeed, the Benedictine concept of poverty as communal sharing is precisely the point Jesus was making in Matthew 6 when he told us not to be preoccupied pursuing the stuff that rots or gets moth-eaten or can be stolen. Instead, we are to invest in the kingdom, because the only riches we can take with us when we go is our investment in the lives of others. It's well said that no hearse pulls a U-Haul. But it might lead a parade of folks whose lives have been touched by one who did not lose the use of her heart and her hands and whose ear remained free of the waxy buildup of stuff so that she could hear the needs of others.

We don't have to enter the monastery to practice what Benedict teaches. There are many ways in which we can demonstrate Christian stewardship and communal ownership of material goods. My daughter and son-in-law replaced their car with a bus pass and participation in a citywide car-sharing program; whenever they need a car they request the use of one from the co-op to which they belong, use it for a few hours, and return it to a designated location for someone else to use. This is not much different from the concept of a library—a service that even most churches offer. But what if our church communities also had "libraries" of tools and other items that people need occasionally but do not need to own? I was grateful when the head of maintenance at our church lent me the church's special wrench to loosen a stubborn gas-supply pipe in our fireplace. Since I had been at my wits' end before he offered the wrench, I was so elated by the good results that I told him I would have to purchase one of these gadgets. He wisely reminded me that I would hardly ever need one, and if I needed one in the future, it would still be available in the church's tool shed.

Certainly we could hold each other more accountable for our consumption of material goods and our stewardship of resources. When I was in Kenya, I witnessed a *harambee*. This Swahili word literally means "pulling together," and in this instance it designated a fundraising party hosted by a prominent Kenyan lawyer on behalf of a college student who needed money to attend seminary in the United States. But it's not as simple as mere fundraising: as the student explained to me, those who invested in his seminary education would, in a virtual sense, be with him during his years in the United States; he would be held accountable for the stewardship of these resources while studying and for the contribution of his training to the community when he returned.

Of course, we don't have to host a harambee to foster this communal sensibility. Years ago, when Apple began producing personal computers, one day I raved about the features of the latest Mac that I coveted while a friend prepared a meal for us in her kitchen. Finally she stopped peeling potatoes, looked up, and asked, "And how will this serve the kingdom of God?" I never purchased *that* computer, and I thank my friend for her gentle reminder.

Jesus reminds his hearers that possessions can give a false sense of security (Luke 12:13–21), can keep a person from accepting the rabbi's call to follow (Mark 10:17–22), and can even blind us to kingdom priorities (Matt. 26:6–16). This outlook on our possessions is something that Benedictine monasticism has cultivated with an eschatological perspective and the constant awareness of our mortality. Though, as Columba Stewart points out, *memento mori* ("be mindful of dying") is found only rarely in the *Rule of*

St. Benedict, passages such as *RB* 4.47 do call us back to the reality of our human situation, much as God reprimanded the rich farmer in Jesus's parable: "Day by day remind yourself that you are going to die."[4] As Stewart says, "Awareness of mortality exerts a unique power to focus the mind and heart on essentials."[5] Certainly that is the message of the apostle Paul in the latter half of Romans 8, in the light of which Michael Casey remarks that Benedict "repeatedly sets before the monks the prospect of heaven. In later centuries, devotion to heaven will become one of the distinguishing marks of Benedictine monasticism. Without such an eschatological perspective . . . monastic life will never gain its specific character."[6] Indeed, a continual reminder of our mortality and of the coming reign of God in all its fullness helps to shape monastic simplicity, as it must ours, so that Christians can practice the bumper-sticker imperative "Live simply so that others may simply live."

5

OBEDIENCE

Objectifying Providence

As monasticism developed, adherents made commitments to what were called the "counsels of perfection" or the "evangelical [i.e., gospel] vows." These three vows were chastity, obedience, and poverty. They were features of the Christian life that were meant to take one a step further toward spiritual maturity than the "ordinary" lay Christian—a bifurcation that was criticized by Protestant Reformers. They were distinguished from "precepts"—those rules by which every follower of Jesus must live in order to attain eternal life. The evangelical counsels were for those who wanted to go the "extra mile" in their life of faith. These were folks who resonated with Jesus's response to the rich young ruler who had kept all the commandments: he should go a step further and sell his possessions, give the proceeds to the poor, and follow Jesus. Thus, commitments such as poverty and celibacy would allow one to press on toward perfection, unhindered by passions that distract one from the kingdom of God. Today's monks would disown this two-tiered concept of the soul's progress, though they commit themselves to a life that is different from what the rest of us usually experience.

Benedictines are unique in that the three vows professed are to obedience, stability, and *conversatio moralis* (sometimes understood as "conversion of life," though it is a Latin phrase that is difficult to translate into English). Implicit within these are the other two evangelical vows of chastity and poverty.

Chastity is not mentioned much these days. When I was growing up, we heard that it was the name Sonny and Cher gave their daughter. (It's better than "Moon Unit," I suppose.) But beyond that and an occasional word association with "belt," we don't hear the term very often. It's our loss, particularly in Christian circles. We settle for teaching a secular concept of abstinence—the willful wrestling of lust to a truce. Over against abstinence, chastity is a virtue that substitutes divine grace for human willpower, virtuous character for isolated moments in near sexual encounters, and a holistic emphasis for a focus on one narrow aspect of human experience.[1] Rather than practicing and recommending random acts of abstinence, Christians need to make chastity more respectable in today's culture.

The same gap often shows up in connection with that other evangelical vow—obedience. It's almost a dirty word outside of military schools. But it really needs to be part of the Christian's vocabulary.

The monk's *surrender* of his will to others sounds harsh to the modern Western ear, which places a premium on individual autonomy and freedom of choice. Yet we must understand that the monk freely chooses to make the vow of obedience to his superior and that this vow is made as a means to a spiritual end. Ultimately, obedience will not destroy the monk's liberty; it will strengthen it. It will provide opportunities for God to work in the individual's life in ways that would not be possible if one were at the mercy of his own whims. Thomas Merton put it well when he described his entrance into the monastic life: "So Brother Matthew locked the gate behind me and I was enclosed in the four walls of my new freedom."[2]

Good Bible-believing, disciple-minded Protestants know this. It's a principle Jesus emphasized in John 8:31–32 (even though we usually hear only the latter verse, ripped out of context). To paraphrase: If you abide, live in, obey the words of Jesus, then you are his disciple. And *then* you will know (experientially) the truth of Jesus's words, and obedience to his truth will set you free.

This came home to me in my more fundamentalist, take-the-Bible-literally high school days. For some reason, in the middle of a PE game of flag football, Rocky (yes—leather coat, razor-cut hair, pointed-toe black shoes) did not like something I had said or done during the game. He came up to me and hit me in the jaw (which to this day pops when the dentist tells me to open so she can check the alignment of my joints). Naive enough to think that Jesus meant what he said about "turning the other cheek," I simply stood there staring at Rocky (probably more out of pain, disbelief, and fear than radical discipleship) until we all resumed play. Afterward, as we showered and dressed for our next class, Rocky came over to my locker and simply said, "I'm sorry that I hit you." From that day on Rocky and I got along fine. Abiding in—or obeying—Jesus's words (regardless of the primary motivation) rather than retaliating tit for tat had literally freed Rocky and me from a cycle of revenge and mutual animosity. And I knew that day the truth of Jesus's words about turning the other cheek.

In a similar way, the monk obeys in order to be freer than he would be if he did not. But we must further explore the Benedictine brand of obedience.

First, it is a *"mutual* obedience" (the title of chapter 71 in the *Rule*). It involves consulting others, seeking advice, expressing desires, giving feedback, inviting initiative—all for the common good. The way of the world is often a one-way hierarchy that demands conformity. But, like Jesus, Benedict insists that it must not be so among his monks. Just as the apostle Paul commanded husbands and wives to "submit to *one another* out of reverence for Christ" (Eph. 5:21—the topic sentence for the rest of Ephesians 5), so the members of Benedict's community—whether juniors or seniors—are to practice a mutual obedience that fosters harmony in the monastic household.

This is healthy. It encourages a sense of *co*responsibility before the Lord. I often experienced just the opposite at an image-conscious college where I once taught. When decisions had to be made about bringing speakers to campus, for example, the president did not invite consultation with those professors whose expertise was the speaker's but responded that he *was* the college. This was motivated by a desire to impose uniformity in light of anticipated feedback from outsiders, rather than to encourage harmonious agreement among community members so as to engender a sense of coresponsibility. Not only would Benedict's vision be healthier for the community and for the leader's physical and emotional health, but, as we will see, it requires an atmosphere of trust that was lacking at this college.

One thing Benedict did have in common with those who rule heavy-handedly was a dislike of "murmuring." He understood that grumbling that lies just below the surface ("in the heart"—*RB* 5.17–18) can pollute a community's esprit de corps. But he also understood that ruling as "the Gentiles" do only exacerbates such grumbling. This becomes clear when chapter 5 of the *Rule*—on obedience—is read in light of chapter 72 on "the good zeal of monks": quoting Romans 12:10, Benedict defines the good zeal that monks are to foster:

> They should each try to be the first to show respect to the other, supporting with greatest patience one another's weaknesses of body or behavior, and earnestly competing in obedience to one another. No one is to pursue what he judges better for himself, but instead, what he judges better for someone else. To their fellow monks they show the pure love of brothers; to God, loving fear; to their abbot, unfeigned and humble love. (*RB* 72.4–10)

In other words, mutual obedience flows from the love of God that is mediated through the loving respect shown by brothers and sisters for each other.

Murmuring is thus obviated. It is obviated when those assigned KP for the week receive an extra portion of drink and bread an hour before mealtime so they can serve the community without grumbling at mealtime (*RB* 35.12–13). It is avoided when the abbot so arranges mealtimes according to the demands of each season that community members go about their work without "justifiable grumbling" (since Benedict has nothing against *legitimate* complaints; *RB* 41.5). Murmuring does not accompany service if additional help is available when it is needed to serve guests in the kitchen (*RB* 53.18). And complaints about the "color or coarseness" of monastic clothing are mitigated when the abbot pays careful attention to fit (*RB* 55.7–8). Benedict's *Rule* covers specifics such as these that put feet on the admonition in Hebrews 10:24 (NASB) "to *consider* how to stimulate one another to love and good deeds." I suspect that if more Christian institutions paid as much respect to their members as Benedict insists upon in the concrete, there would be the kind of competition to obey one another that Benedict suggests in chapter 72.

When I stop grumbling, I am in a position to listen. In fact, obedience is the aim of listening. (Interestingly, in Latin the same word, *oboedire*, can mean "to obey" or "to listen to.") I hear the needs of my brother or my sister, or I hear God's call through my Christian sibling, and I respond in obedience.

I became aware of this in practice every evening at dinner in the monastery. Benedict's *Rule* (chapter 38) provides for reading at table. That is, a monk is assigned to read aloud installments of a selected book while the rest eat their dinner in silence. (It's a wonderful spalike luxury to have someone read to you while you eat.) This means that if you want the salt and pepper that happen to be halfway down the table, you'd better hope that someone anticipates your desire or can read your spontaneously invented sign language. But not to worry: monks have been trained to obey; they "hear" the silent request and respond quickly.

Once again, it's a matter of training. If you eat in silence every evening, you learn to anticipate the needs and concerns of those at the table. One morning at breakfast with a few Episcopalians after midweek morning Eucharist I was gently reminded of my lack of training. (I often worship with Episcopalians to get a "second opinion.") While I focused intently on my platter of eggs, bacon, and toast, Mark—ready to consume a healthy bowl of oatmeal—quietly suggested, "Dennis, why don't you pass your brother the brown sugar?" I was being trained, for relational virtues like obedience and humility can only be learned in community. This is why Benedict insists that monks cannot become hermits in the desert until they have "come through the test of living in a monastery for a long time," so that "thanks to the help and guidance of many, they are now trained to fight against the devil"—"to grapple single-handed with the vices of body and mind" (*RB* 1.3–5). It's difficult to practice obedience and humility when you're the only one around. Every time I interact with someone I have another opportunity to hear and obey my brother's or sister's call—even if it is not verbalized. In the end, obedience is responsiveness.

But ultimately I am being trained for more than a readiness to hear and obey the brother's or sister's request. In the end, I want to be ready to hear *God's* word to *me* on *this* day. As in responding to a request for salt rather than for sugar, specificity is everything when it comes to obedience, particularly when we are responding to a divine request. For instance, if Mary had been given options she might have chosen adoption.

Folks like Mary and monks remind me how far I have to go in my ability to hear and obey God. It is involvement in the *coenobium*—the common life—that makes it possible for me to grow into a deeper awareness of God's will for me. This is why the oft-heard sentiment of Protestants that it's just "Jesus and me" is dangerously misguided. Left to myself (even with Jesus), I am easily deceived and very unreliable. Of course, Protestants *should* know this, and they *have* taught it. It was the concern of Dietrich Bonhoeffer, who warned against the individual who imposes his "wish-dream" on the community—such a one "loves his dream of a community more than the Christian community itself [and] becomes a destroyer of the latter," for such an imposition is a symptom of attempts at self-justification.[3]

At the beginning of his *Rule* (in the first chapter), Benedict describes four kinds of monks. The former two he likes; the latter two he despises. One of the despised he calls "sarabaites." These are disobedient monks who "lie to God by their tonsure," who "pen themselves up in their own sheepfolds, not the Lord's," and whose law is "what they like to do, whatever strikes their fancy": "anything they believe in and choose, they call holy; anything they dislike, they consider forbidden" (*RB* 1.6–9). Appropriately, after introducing the second kind of despised monk, Benedict launches into a relatively long chapter on the qualities of the abbot, whom the good monk must obey.

For Benedictines there is no monasticism without an abbot (or prioress in women's monasteries). The abbot (from the Aramaic word *abba*, for "father") is the representative of Christ to the community. Nevertheless, the monk's promised obedience to this Christ-stand-in does not mean that the monk is at the mercy of a tyrant's whim, any more than it implies that the abbot should command something that would deviate from the Lord's instructions (*RB* 2.2–4).

Brother Gene had been a marine before he became a monk, and he once told me, "Joining the monastery is a lot like joining the Marines. It's just that the motivation is different." Actually, he knew better. Obedience to the superior in an abbey is much different from obedience to a drill sergeant or general in the military. For one thing, just as 1 John repeatedly makes clear, in the monastery "obedience is the concrete expression of filiation."[4] That is to say, the *Rule of St. Benedict* does not insist on blind obedience: "for obedience to work, all the parties must be awake." The abbot or prioress is not a police officer; the superior is a caring father, a trusted mother: "Obedience is thus essentially a conversation, an intimate exchange based upon trust that the relationship is life-giving." Obedience—the willingness to listen—is vitiated by mistrust or abuse.[5]

We once had to hide a former student of mine from her pastor—literally. We feared for her life. While in college, she was attending a church in Illinois of which her church pastor back home in Maine did not approve. He insisted that because he was her pastor, he had absolute authority over her decisions and activities. The student's mother was under his authority to the extent that she threatened to withhold funds for tuition and to disown her daughter. The pastor intimated that he would pay a visit, presumably to make the young woman obey his orders or to bring her home. The abuse this student experienced led to her "disobedience," precisely because this relationship was not based on trust nor was it "life-giving." In this case, the lack of obedience was a concrete expression of *disaffiliation* (in the literal sense of the term, albeit with a feminine nuance).

During a forty-five-minute phone conversation that the pastor initiated, when I asked him if he was involved in any kind of ministerial association, he replied, "No, they're all liberal."

"Then are you in some relationship of mutual accountability?" I asked.

Arrogantly, he insisted, "I'm only accountable to God." It was clear that this was a situation of "blind obedience," though while obedience was being demanded of the parishioner, the blindness in this case was attributable to the pastor. Though he would never have tolerated the advice of a Roman Catholic monastic, this church leader would have been well advised by Benedict, who reminds the abbot that because he will have to give an account at the final judgment for his disciples' souls as well as his own, he must always be aware of his own weaknesses and limitations (*RB* 2.37–40). And as I've already pointed out, those are discovered in community with others.

Of course, Benedict is clear that abbots rule. (This might inspire a marketable T-shirt among monastics!) But again, this is like the parental authority that the apostle Paul specifies in Ephesians 6:4. Paul warns fathers not to "provoke [their] children to anger." In a similar manner, Benedict instructs abbots to "hate faults but love the brothers" and to "use prudence and avoid extremes" when he must punish them; "otherwise, by rubbing too hard to remove the rust, he may break the vessel" (*RB* 64.11–12).

In fact, the qualities of the abbot that the *Rule* prescribes ensure the wisest and most charitable spiritual direction of those whose formation is his responsibility. The abbot must teach in word and deed. Above all, he must be an example. He is not a teacher in the sense of a scholar or professor who passes on information in a classroom through lecture. He is the one who has experienced firsthand the wisdom of the monastic tradition, and with the qualifications of charity and wisdom (not necessarily intellectual brilliance or academic achievement), he assists his disciples in their total personal conversion. He is the director of their formation, not merely the imparter of information.

Before I had ever read the *Rule*, I saw this characterization of the abbot in action the first time I visited a monastery. At the end of the meal, after the abbot had led the community in the prayer of dismissal, Abbot Denis made a beeline for the door of the kitchen to initiate the clearing of tables. I tried to think of any pastors in the Protestant churches I had attended who made a similar dart for the dishwater at the end of a potluck dinner, but, sadly, I could remember none.

Benedict insists that the abbot must show equal love to all his monks, but the wisdom that directs charity does not always mean equal treatment. Here again is the genius of Benedict's rule. The *Rule* leaves enough latitude that the wise abbot must play the crucial role of discerning the spiritual needs of each individual monk in his community, for each one is at a different stage on his journey toward God. With discretion he makes adjustments for each individual. (Though modern-day monastics are concerned about dwindling numbers in their communities, at the same time they could not be tempted to adopt the splashy techniques used by some to grow big churches today, for then no abbot could do what the shepherd of every church is technically supposed to do: attend to the needs of each sheep's spiritual development. In fact, the word *dean* comes from the title given to the supervisor appointed to oversee *ten* community members.)

So discernment and discretion are key attributes for the abbot. The abbot is not expected to be omniscient or sinless, and he is to seek the advice of the community much of the time. But since Benedict—recognizing the infinite variety, complexity, and individuality of human beings—did not attempt to regulate everything in advance, the abbot bears the heavy responsibility of exercising discretion in each circumstance and with each individual. Souls are not mass-produced. There is no factory assembly line when it comes to our sanctification. Each Christian disciple has specific needs, potential, temperament, intelligence, and gifts. And the leader of a spiritual community must employ wisdom, patience, good humor, imagination, and a host of other qualities and skills in assisting each one under his or her charge toward spiritual maturity.

This is why the metaphor of *conversation* characterizes the Benedictine interplay of authority and obedience. The monk who is expected to obey has permission to respond with reasons that it might be difficult or impossible to carry out commands: "he should choose the appropriate moment and explain patiently to his superior why he cannot perform the task. This he ought to do without pride, obstinacy, or refusal" (*RB* 68.2–3). This would have been a better approach for the pastor from Maine to have taken with my student; it's certainly a healthy model for our parent-child and employer-employee relationships. After the conversation, the monk (or the child or the worker) might still be expected to carry out the command—not to suit the needs or wishes of the abbot (or parent or boss) but to enhance the community's functioning and facilitate the growth of the obedient one. And "trusting in God's help, [the monk] must in love obey" (*RB* 68.5).

This is exactly what happened at Blue Cloud Abbey when the abbot told Brother Rene that he would be playing the organ to accompany the chanting of psalms during the daily office. I'm sure Brother Rene informed the abbot that he did not know how to play the organ (as he had told me). But the order stood. Rene was given two weeks to learn. He did. The community was well served as he led us in choir. My students and I never would have guessed that he was a novice at the instrument, and Rene never would have discovered what God could enable him to accomplish without his obedience.

Sometimes we grow by obeying and allowing God's grace to work through our obedience. When authority and obedience are exercised in a context of trusting and respectful relations, God's providence can be experienced. As Columba Stewart put it, "Without love, obedience is impossible: Christ, after all, was a beloved son, not a masochist."[6]

In the end, Bob Dylan was right: "Well, it may be the devil or it may be the Lord / But you're gonna have to serve somebody." Obedience to one who fits Benedict's description of the Christ-representative entails unseating other powers and frees us to grow up together as God's children. I have often thought that if a Protestant church used chapter 2 of Benedict's *Rule* as a template in the search for its next pastor, it would be far better off than if it looked primarily for the captivating preacher or charismatic inspirer of numerical and building growth.

Such a servant-leader and the obedience required of disciples go hand in hand. Perhaps *obedience* remains a soiled word today because we lack the kinds of leaders Benedict describes.

But even in our ordinary lives we "have to serve somebody," some institution, some tradition, or some rules. We like to think of ourselves as independent, rugged individuals who make our own rules. But as Brian Taylor reminds us, if we seek God's will for our life every choice we make requires a new obedience. If we decide to remain single, we must follow the rules of temperance in sexual relations. If we decide to be married, we must follow the rules of fidelity. If we don't follow the rules, we and others suffer. Disobedience yields only an illusory freedom.[7]

This is what a friend of mine discovered a few years ago. I had been preaching on a regular basis at a church in Oak Park, Illinois. One of the parishioners had attempted suicide. She failed, but the Saturday morning incident made big news at church the next day. Her husband David (not his real name) asked to meet with me the following day. As we talked over lunch, the story unraveled: his wife had been having an affair, and this suicide attempt was her complicated way of confessing her sin and expressing shame. As David put it, he was immersed in a deep mire. (He used more graphic language.) Their marriage was never restored, and after many doses of counseling and prescription drugs, David was able to remarry. But I remember returning to my office the day we met for lunch thinking, "To this culture faithful monogamy may look boring, but it sure beats what David is experiencing." God has set limits that, like buoys in a channel, keep us and those affected by our actions from getting stuck in the dregs and lead us toward the fulfilling life Christ promised.

In light of David's story, Taylor makes the point well:

> A good example of the freedom gained through obedience is found in family life. Children need attention, money has to be gotten, my wife must be listened to even when I feel my resources drained. Obedience to these limits within the discipline of family life brings with it a certain freedom, which is found in love. Love as a father and as a husband is deeper than any I have ever known, and I know that this has been made possible through the countless acts of obedience to familial limits that I have made over the years: doing this or that because I know that I have to as a father and as a husband. Love without obedience to these limits and rules is a shallow love, unable to really give except when it feels good to do so. . . . I have found that through the limits of obedience I grow beyond the confines of the self with its desires and traps.[8]

Benedict says it well in verse 49 of his prologue: "But as we progress in this way of life and in faith, we shall run on the path of God's commandments, our hearts overflowing with the inexpressible delight of love." Jesus said it even better: "They who have my commandments and keep them are those who love me; and those who love me will be loved by my Father, and I will love them and reveal myself to them" (John 14:21). The sign of love is obedience, whether I am observing the rules of family life, of being a good steward of God's resources, or of working faithfully as an employee. Through such obedience born of love, I risk being converted by the involvement of others in my life to become more than I would be otherwise. Joan Chittister puts it so well: "The whole world, in other words, is an organic whole, a system of interlocking parts meant both to hold me up and to stretch me at the same time. License is an attempt to sabotage the system, to be my own small world, to be my own measure of meaning in life."[9]

6

HUMILITY

Letting Go of the Mask

Brother Gene was a perceptive monk. One day as we were walking down a corridor at Blue Cloud Abbey, for a reason I cannot remember he wagged his finger at me and said, "You like to be in control, don't you?" Translation: "You are not humble."

Humility breaks down our egoistic fantasies and our need to be in control—our need to be the exception. When we are humble we understand that we are not the exception. We are, like it or not, simply part of the human race.

This is why Michael Casey, a Cistercian, titled his book on humility *A Guide to Living in the Truth*.[1] Humility is not selling ourselves short. Nor is it selling ourselves at an inflated price—which is pride, the opposite of humility. Humility requires what Columba Stewart calls "radical self-honesty," achieved at times with the assistance of a spiritual director who helps us to "discern our thoughts."[2] This is not unlike the fifth step of humility in Benedict's *Rule* (*RB* 7.44), when a person "does not conceal from his abbot any sinful thoughts entering his heart, or any wrongs committed in secret, but rather confesses them humbly." It is grounded in a realistic acceptance of who we are—our unchangeable past, our inherited DNA, our innate gifts and aptitudes, our failures and successes, our weaknesses and our strengths, and our relationships with others and with God. As Casey says, the alternative is "a life built on radical untruth."[3]

The humble person is the one who has ditched the mask—not feigning with an "aw shucks" response to merited praise, and not joining the Pharisee in the public square who boasts that he is not like "those sinners." It is the person who knows he cannot change at least four facts about our human situation: we are not divine; we are creatures; we are sinners; and we are "stalled human beings" (i.e., people with all the "liabilities of our personal history").[4]

Benedict stressed humility because he understood that it is essential if a community is to flourish. The one who believes that the rules do not apply to her is the one who cannot respect or deal gently with the rest of the human race, who must labor under the rules. It reminds me of the independently wealthy couple my wife and I drove to the Philadelphia airport so that they could catch their flight to Hawaii. As we slogged along in the morning rush hour, one of them asked, "What is all this traffic?" When I replied, "It's people going to work," the other one remarked, with every bit of reverence she could muster, "God bless 'em."

Pride makes us unapproachable. It destroys community—or it draws people into an unhealthy alliance of reproach and gossip about the egomaniac in their midst. But if a person possesses a realistic assessment of who she is, whence she's come, and where her place is in the scheme of things, she has a good chance of accepting others for who they are, whence they've come, and what their place is in the scheme of things—without necessarily approving of all that is included in the assessment.[5]

Though for Benedict humility was a strength of character, these days it, like obedience, is not always appreciated. This is nothing new, of course, since humility was not treated as a virtue in the writings of the ancients like Plato. But it's particularly demoted in a culture where, as one *Los Angeles Times* editorial warned, it is unwise to use your turn signal to change lanes on the freeway for fear of encouraging the car behind you to speed up. Not so for Benedict. Humility is *pro*moted in the *Rule*; in fact, it is the subject of the longest chapter (about 8 percent of the entire *Rule*).

Chapter 7 outlines the ladder of humility in twelve steps. In fact, at first it appears to be a "twelve-step program" for attaining humility. Unlike the self-help books and New Age promotions of self-improvement, it shares with recovery programs an emphasis on recognizing our shortcomings. But as Casey and Stewart rightly have pointed out, the steps are descriptive, not prescriptive or programmatic. You do not have to complete step 4 before going on to step 5. In fact, they do not really represent a sequence except for the first and final steps: the monk must *begin* with the fear of God and *finish* by manifesting humility in every aspect of his life. Getting from one to the other over the course of several decades of monastic life is a journey through the other ten descriptive milestones, which measure progress rather than cause it. As Casey reminds us, "Humility is a very slow business if it is authentic."[6] It's another instance of a spirituality that is not in a hurry.

It is interesting that in the *Rule* the chapter on humility follows the chapters on obedience and "restraint of speech."[7] Like obedience and poverty, humility is an exercise in giving up my own will. It's all tied to the self-emptying that the apostle Paul talks about in Philippians 2. In different ways, obedience, limiting speech, poverty, and humility all involve the eradication of self-will and self-centeredness.

Actually, Benedict comes down pretty hard at this point. The seventh step of humility "is that a man not only admits with his tongue but is also convinced in his heart that he is inferior to all and of less value" (*RB* 7.51). Understandably, this does not set well with a culture that is afflicted with self-esteemia. But Stewart reminds us that in describing this step Benedict is moving from Psalm 22:6 ("I am a worm, and not human") to his paraphrased rendition of Psalm 88:15 ("I was exalted, then I was humbled and overwhelmed with confusion") to Psalm 119:71 ("It is good for me that I was humbled, so that I might learn your statutes"). In other words, we go "from a false sense of self to painful self-recognition, which is the only place where listening to God can happen."[8]

Before self-righteous Protestants get on Benedict's case, they need to take a second look (or a *first* look in most cases) at chapter 15 of the Scots Confession: "When we have done all things we must fall down and unfeignedly confess that we are unprofitable servants [an allusion to Jesus's assessment of his disciples in Luke 17:10]. Therefore, whoever boasts of the merits of his own works or puts his trust in works of supererogation, boasts of what does not exist, and puts his trust in damnable idolatry." Benedict has nothing on the Presbyterian John Knox.

The Christian fact and the realistic assessment of our situation is that we are sinners, even *while*, as the Scots Confession reminds us, God "accepts our imperfect obedience as if it were perfect, and covers our works, which are defiled with many stains, with the righteousness of his Son." This is Luther's *simul justus et peccator*—at the same time I am righteous and a sinner. Still, we moderns tend to major on the former appraisal and minor on the latter.

A good self-assessment can be had if we pay close attention to the characters with which we identify in Jesus's parables. For example, I never understood Jesus's parable about the equal wages that vineyard workers were paid regardless of the time of day they punched the clock (Matt. 20:1–16). While I was humble enough to admit that I would not have shown up with the overly conscientious 6 a.m. zealots, I always identified with the workers who got there at 9 a.m. (I like my coffee and paper in the morning). And we who got there early in the day were being treated unjustly from a human perspective when we were paid the same amount as the loafing latecomers. As a result I thought the parable was about justice and injustice; but then it still didn't make any sense. Finally, it dawned on me: Jesus's point was not that I got there early while less responsible individuals and lazy welfare cheats showed up just before quitting time. Jesus's point was that *I* got there at 5 p.m., that *I* do not deserve the grace of a wage equivalent to those who have worked far longer and harder, but that *I* am indeed a recipient of God's unmerited grace just like everyone else, no matter how long and hard they work. The parable isn't about justice after all; it's about grace.

This realization is much like Donald Miller's awakening after a day of protesting President Bush:

> More than my questions about the efficacy of social action were my questions about my own motives. Do I want social justice for the oppressed, or do I just want to be known as a

socially active person? I spend 95 percent of my time thinking about myself anyway. I don't have to watch the evening news to see that the world is bad, I only have to look at myself. . . . I was the very problem I had been protesting. I wanted to make a sign that read "I AM THE PROBLEM!"

. . . I talk about love, forgiveness, social justice; I rage against American materialism in the name of altruism, but have I even controlled my own heart? The overwhelming majority of the time I spend thinking about myself, pleasing myself, reassuring myself, and when I am done there is nothing to spare for the needy. Six billion people live in this world, and I can only muster thoughts for one. Me.[9]

I cannot plead innocent. I have contributed to the sum total of misery in the world. As Stewart puts it so well, "The awareness of our own frailty always exceeds what we can know of another's. Therefore we have no choice but to 'believe with deep feeling of heart' that we are inferior to all despite our backgrounds, our skills or our education."[10] Or, as Casey incisively remarks, "I have more evidence of crime against myself than I have for any other human being. My conscience accuses me directly of so much malice, whereas I know only by hearsay of the evil done by others. To be humble before God is to know that I am blameworthy."[11]

Of course, the flip side is this: self-emptying humility places us in the right posture to receive grace. Humility opens us up. As Casey defines it, humility is "the capacity for receiving grace and the gift of final salvation . . : a willingness to be saved, an openness to God's action, an assent to the mysterious processes by which God's plan is realized in the hearts of human beings." Said differently, humility is rooted in trust.

I live near the southern California beaches, and occasionally we see or hear about rescues of those who have been swept out by a riptide. Lifeguards promptly assess the situation and rush out to save the person who is struggling futilely against the stubborn current. In order to be saved, the swimmer must stop fighting the current and the lifeguard and give in. The problem is that by the time the two get back to the curious crowd on the beach, the lifeguard—the one who can save himself and another—is lauded and the rescued is written off as a fool for ignoring the warning signs of a rip current or for being a weakling. It's humiliating to be saved, because it requires that I acknowledge my enslavement to narcissism and the riptide pull of tendencies that I prefer not to admit—even to myself. But if I persist in believing the inflated percentage of my self-approval rating, then I will never admit that I really need God.

Such Christian humility is not the same thing as low self-esteem or poor self-image. It is simply the refusal to be deluded by the lie that I am guiltless: "Empowered by the intensity of God's unconditional love for me, I find it possible to demolish my defenses and to admit the truth of my condition. There is nothing in my constitution or personal history that would give me any confidence in my own competence to bring my life to a happy conclusion."[12] This is why Benedict begins the ladder of humility with mindfulness of the fear of God. Like obedience, humility involves confidence or trust in God and in those with whom God has chosen to place us.

Only those who have a realistic assessment of their worth can truly trust God. If we cultivate an inflated sense of our existence, we will find it difficult to trust the apostle Paul's insistence that God is working for the benefit of those who are called and chosen by God. (This is a point that Calvinistic-leaning Protestants have pushed, though sometimes extending it a bit too far, out-Calvining Calvin.) For instance, we might mistakenly believe that our present circumstances are indispensable for God to get kingdom work done. Yet God's call to a less prestigious position or a less attractive assignment in life might be part of a larger picture that only God can appreciate. It requires trust in divine providence to accept the fact that what appears less prestigious from a human perspective is precisely what gives me my worth from the only wide-angle perspective that ultimately and accurately counts. I have to be humble enough to admit that I am often fooled by appearances; I have to have a robust faith that God's will is always to our benefit despite appearances.[13]

This trust in what God is up to is expressed by John's eschatological insistence that "we will be like him [Christ] *for* we shall see him as he is" (1 John 3:2). I could never figure this one out: how is seeing Jesus going to *cause* me to be like him? I took the "for" in the sentence as causal—the latter will result in the former. But the word is not causal; it's circumstantial. It's as if someone had described to me in detail how well Andres Segovia plays the guitar. Trusting my source of information, I then spend years practicing to play like Segovia. Finally, Segovia comes to my town, and I see and hear him play for the first time. Now I realize that I play like Segovia, because I now see and hear him for myself. During all these years of practice I have had to trust my informant that I was indeed developing a style and capability like Segovia's, until finally I no longer have to trust; I see for myself what I have become.

The crucial difference in the analogy is this: I not only trust my informant about who Christ is (namely, the canonical Gospels as they have been faithfully transmitted and proclaimed by the church), but I also trust that the Spirit of Christ is doing this work in my life, transforming me from glory into glory, doing a work underneath the scaffolding of my daily existence that, if yielded to and obeyed, will one eschatological day reveal a pleasant surprise—I'll look like Jesus Christ. Through the process of sanctification, I will have been refashioned into the very image of God, who is Jesus Christ (Col. 1:15)—often even without my awareness that this was taking place. Calvin himself defined sanctification as the process of becoming human again—of being renewed in the image of the One who made us in the first place.[14]

This is good news for those tempted to overvaluation and those resigned to underevaluation of their worth. In both cases it is difficult to trust the unconditional love of God—the only kind we can have. Only those who are humble enough to realize that God does not love us because something we have cultivated attracts his love, and only those who are humble enough to trust that God still loves them when they know how unlovable they are—only these can discover the love of God that itself determines our worth. This is because God's love is not a commodity that can be bought or bartered.

Such trust that accompanies humility must characterize not only our relationship with God but also our relationship with those in whose company we are being sanctified. I will take up this subject further in a subsequent chapter, but for now let me say that this is where the Benedictine vows of stability (staying in the community to which God has called you) and *conversatio moralis* (daily turning to God) come into play. Whether the community is a monastery, a family, or a church, by remaining in the same community day after day, we are nearly *forced* to become humble. I cannot continue to wear the mask that hides my true self if I am with the same people on a regular basis. (Said differently, church-hopping is a useful practice if you want to nurture your pride.) When a group of folks are committed to mutual spiritual development, we can be transparent and vulnerable because we can trust that others will have our best interests at heart as they speak the truth in love to us. They will know us as we are and will lovingly force us to arrive at the same knowledge.

There are times in our communities when a false kind of humility is encouraged to cover up the incompetence of those who insist on our patience and understanding.[15] An adherent of Benedict's *Rule* would not settle for this. For one thing, all have a role to play in the community according to the *Rule*, and superiors as well as those underneath them must fulfill their responsibilities with integrity. For another thing, if a community member is truly humble, she will be truthful about her own gifts and abilities, and she will act responsibly when the occasion demands it. If that means boldly speaking out against incompetence, then the community will be better for it in the long run. If it means taking the initiative when a job needs to be done or done well, then the one who is gifted to lead or assist in the project must do so. True humility is not milquetoast acquiescence nor fearful timidity.

Sometimes people are not humble enough to acknowledge the abilities of others or to allow the gifted to play the role they should because they themselves feel threatened and insecure. As a result, the community does not benefit, and the proud insecure fellow will not learn from those more capable. The *Rule* will have none of this. This comes out most clearly in Benedict's teaching about rank, for seniority in the monastery has nothing to do with age or degree or title or pedigree. Instead, it is based on the time that one entered the community (*RB* 63.5–8). My neighbors leaned on this principle, for example, when they balked at my admonition that their permanently parked vehicle precluded anyone else from using the community parking space. They quickly put me in my place: not only did they own a production company and a mortgage company (trumping my advanced age, four graduate degrees, and publication record, I suppose), but they reminded me that my wife and I were the newest residents of our four-house association. They pulled rank in accord with the *Rule of Benedict* (I'm guessing without realizing it). But this is where the *Rule* becomes even more interesting (and would have supported my helpful suggestion about sharing the community parking space).

Not only does the order of entry do away with privilege based on social conventions, but Benedict also insists that the seniors must sometimes take the advice of the juniors: "The reason why we have said *all* should be called for counsel [about important monastery business] is that the Lord often reveals what is better to the younger" (*RB* 3.3). Even the selection of the abbot is not determined by seniority, even Benedict's definition of seniority. Instead, in the chapter that gives guidance for choosing an abbot, the *Rule* emphasizes that "goodness of life and wisdom in teaching" are to be the criteria for choosing the abbot, "*even if* he is the *last* in community rank" (RB, 64.2). Columba Stewart finds this aspect of Benedictine monastic life revolutionary: "The countercultural witness of monasticism to the essential dignity of every person expressed in Benedict's deliberate rejection of conventional forms of social ordering, remains one of the most important gifts of monasticism to Church and society."[16]

The bottom line is that only the humble will allow themselves to be formed by those with whom they live. This is why the *Rule* connects humility with restraint of speech, obedience, and stability.

And what will be formed? People who are at home with themselves. People who live in truth—in the truth that their worth comes from the fact that they are creatures of God for whom Christ died, not from having their name painted on a parking space.

Paradoxically, pride not only will keep us from recognizing the true source of our dignity but will also keep us from admitting our biodegradable fragility, sinful liabilities, and naked ordinariness—prerequisite admissions if we are to allow ourselves to be transformed by God's grace.

One day as my wife and I were taking a walk, one woman approached another and exclaimed, "Is that *you*?" I immediately said to my wife, "What an unusual question. What if the person she's approaching answers, 'No, it's not I. I know you thought it was, but it's not I'?" It's a strange question when you're approaching someone on the street, but the more I think about it, the more it strikes me that it's not a strange question if you're cultivating humility. One Benedictine might approach another and ask, "Is that you?" And the one climbing the ladder of humility might answer, "Not yet, but someday."

7

HOSPITALITY

The Guest as Christ

When Benedict gets around to discussing different ways in which the monastery and the world meet, one of the important topics with which he deals is the reception of guests (chapter 53). He immediately states the overarching principle: "*All* guests who present themselves are to be welcomed as Christ, for he himself will say: I was a stranger and you welcomed me" (*RB* 53.1, quoting Matt. 25:35).

This welcome goes beyond the simple handshake. The monks are to meet the guest "with all the courtesy of love," marked by prayer, the kiss of peace, and the humble adoration of a bow, so that "Christ is adored because he is indeed welcomed in them" (*RB* 53.7). Now, I have never been received quite so elaborately, but I have been made to feel at home in the monastery as soon as my presence is made known.

Not only is the guest received with joy, but once his "status" is determined, he is to be received "as is," whether rich or poor. Nowhere does Benedict direct his monks to exchange greetings on the basis of titles (with the exception of the monk addressing the abbot). Titles are not important; in fact, presumably they are not to be mentioned. How similar to the warnings against partiality in the book of James (2:1-13), and how embarrassingly dissimilar to the worldly infatuation we often demonstrate toward the celebrity or success story who shows up in our church sanctuary. Again, working from Jesus's warnings in Matthew 25, Benedict reminds us that Christ is "more particularly" received in the poor and the pilgrims than he is in the rich and the famous (*RB* 53.15).

It would be interesting if the incarnation had taken place in twenty-first-century North America instead of first-century Palestine. Jesus may have been as poorly received in and attractive to our megachurches as he was in the "megasynagogues" and temple of his own people. After all, we'd have to extend the right hand of fellowship to a homeless man who had a reputation for hobnobbing with the winebibbers and tax collectors. At best, we might show him hospitality as one of our "see-how-we-minister-to-the-poor" trophies.

If we could genuinely practice Benedict's brand of hospitality, welcoming each guest to our churches as the visitation of Christ, it might transform our guests as well as us. Instead of making the other into my image, I am invited to see the other as one who is made in God's image and for whom Jesus Christ died.

I will never forget the most humble and courageous act of hospitality extended to my six students and me after we had been at Blue Cloud Abbey for one week of our ten-day "field trip." Each Thursday the Blue Cloud monks would gather as a community in private before vespers and Mass to participate in a ritual of communal reconciliation, confessing and forgiving those attitudes and actions that had negatively affected community life in recent days. After Mass they concluded this communal celebration by processing to the basement dining hall for *hors d'oeuvres* and a buffet dinner. It was a highlight of the week, even for guests.

This particular Thursday, after breakfast, the abbot called us into his office and told us how much he had appreciated our presence and participation in the monastery's daily life. He then asked if any of us would like to offer our reflections on the scripture to be read at Mass that evening. Two of my students—one male and one female—jumped at the chance. Only later did I explain to them what an act of hospitality this had been: for the presiding abbot to have asked two Protestant college students (and one a female) was a risk that many Protestants would not reciprocate.

But Benedictine hospitality did not end there. After the two students had delivered brief but poignant reflections on the texts, the abbot responded in a manner that truly astounded me. After we had invaded their house for a week, living in guest quarters that rivaled a Hampton Inn, eating three hearty meals each day, and munching on all the treats the monks had stashed for us in our guest kitchen, the abbot said, "We need to thank these students for coming to us. By their presence in our midst they have challenged us to examine ourselves to see whether or not we live the life we profess." Then he invited any other community members to share their thoughts on the students' visit, and several monks expressed similar sentiments. The dinner celebration that night after the Mass was the crowning point of what had truly been an *agape* meal.[1]

I have often wondered what our churches would be like if we extended the same humble hospitality to the visitors who show up week after week. What a contrast to my visit to the evangelical church my daughter often attended during her college days. Needing to head for the airport immediately after church to return home, I toted my pilot's bag and canvas briefcase to the room where the college class would be meeting and to which we would be returning after the first worship service. Since the high schoolers used the same Sunday school classroom during the first hour, I suggested that my daughter inform one of the adult leaders so that he would be aware that this was my luggage perched by the coat rack and keep an eye on it for me. As he approached me, his first words were (with a smile on his face, of course; we evangelicals are always "nice," if nothing else!), "Could you open the bags so that I can see what's inside?"

Dressed in my Sunday finest, I explained my situation—that I had been a theology professor at the local college for the past decade and a half and that my daughter was a participating member of this church. "You can understand," he said (with a smile). "We can't be too careful."

As I accommodated his fears of a hidden bomb and unzipped the bags to expose my dirty laundry, books, and papers, I retorted (without a smile and, no doubt, in an irritated tone that revealed I was in danger of losing a month's worth of progress in sanctification), "I *don't* understand, and if you came to my church we would not ask a Christian brother to do this."

Indeed, we can't be too careful to show humble hospitality with "all the courtesy of love." Call them naive, but more than once I have heard of the Blue Cloud monks' being "taken" by a guest; they would rather err on the side of welcoming each guest as Christ, perhaps implanting a seed of grace that might one day grow into a life-changing organism, than to put themselves first.

I suppose, though, that the high school overseer could have appealed to Benedict's caution in his exhortations to receive guests: the monk must beware of the "delusions of the devil" (who probably *does* wear khaki slacks and a classic, two-button navy sports jacket) and not allow the routine of the monastery to be unduly compromised (*RB* 53.5). The abbot, who would have washed the guest's hands and, along with the rest of the community, the guest's feet when he entered, can break a fast for the sake of a guest. But beyond that, provision should be made for a separate guest kitchen (along with two attending brothers) so guests do not "disturb the brothers when they present themselves at unpredictable hours" (53.16). And one is to speak to a guest only when bidden; if a brother meets or sees a guest in the monastery, "he asks for a blessing and continues on his way, explaining that he is not allowed to speak with a guest" (53.23–24).

As in many other areas, so here—Benedictines don't practice the letter of Benedict's rule, but they do observe its spirit. The point is this: the monks can best attend to the needs of a guest if the house is functioning as it should. Part of this has to do with the subtle influence the fallen world can have on the Christian community. This is a concern that resonates with Protestants, who have always been concerned, particularly in their fundamentalist incarnations, to "keep the boat in the water without letting the water get into the boat."

Benedict wanted to make sure that newcomers to the monastic life were serious, so he cautioned his monks not to grant them easy entry but to "test the spirits to see if they are from God" (58.1–2, quoting 1 John 4:1). The postulant is to keep knocking at the door for four or five days to dem-

85

onstrate his sincerity (just as a church, which should readily welcome its guests, should test and catechize the one who seeks to join the church in its fellowship and mission). In this way the intentional Christian community is preserved so that it can do best the job that God has assigned it. The postulant must adjust to the community; the community must not let the postulant—or "world"—set the agenda.

Figuratively speaking, maybe we need to recover some sense of making the world wait four or five days outside the gates of our Christian communities. What a contrast to the World War II invasion of Monte Cassino—the rebuilt monastery of Benedict's original that was demolished in the contest between Axis and Allied powers as the latter made the arduous and hard-fought trek to Rome. When my family and I visited the monastery, we learned from the monk who greeted us under the gate labeled PAX that the world refused to wait outside the gate, destroying the monastery with worldly means of bombing raids that were fueled by suspicions of the enemy's intentions. Perhaps if the "world" had had more respect for a Christian community that not all agreed was a threat to the Allies, a treasure would not have been destroyed and the lives of many monks would not have been so disrupted.[2]

Perhaps this metaphorical comparison and the paradoxical dance between showing hospitality to the stranger and keeping the fallen world at bay is best captured in a publisher's blurb for a book entitled *The Two Cities of God: The Church's Responsibility for the Earthly City*:

> The authors assert that the popular slogan of the sixties, "Let the world set the agenda!" must be turned around. The church must set its own agenda in dealing with the world, and that agenda must feature most prominently the church's life in the communion of the Triune God. . . . In each case the

authors agree that the church's greatest witness and service to the world is in the church's day-by-day service to God, both as an institution and in the lives of individual Christians—"a sign and agent of the heavenly city within and for the earthly city."[3]

This is precisely Benedict's point.

But what I find most irritating about practicing Benedictine hospitality when it comes to *receiving* the guest is the *timing* of the guest's appearance. In the spirit of Benedictine hospitality, I used to make a simple request each morning: "Lord, send someone today whom I can serve." But inevitably this someone would show up five minutes before I had to deliver a lecture (the preparation for which really required at least another hour) or before I was dashing off to lunch with a growling stomach. It got to the point that I could not pray this prayer with sincerity—unless I was in greater control of my encounters with guests. And that is precisely the point: the stranger at our "gate" is as unpredictable in his appearance as is Christ. To top it off, this stranger is often the kid who irritates me the most, yet the one whom I must envision as Christ. That often takes not only patience but a *lot* of envisioning!

This came home to me during a conference given to Blue Cloud oblates by our oblate director. (A "conference" is the term Benedictines use for what Protestants would call a "talk" at a retreat.) Brother Benet recited a poem by John L'Heureux entitled "The Trouble with Epiphanies."

> Christ came into my room
> and stood there
> and I was bored to death.
> I had work to do.
> I wouldn't have minded

if he'd been crippled
or something—I do well
with cripples—but he
just stood there, all face,
and with that d—ned guitar.
I didn't ask him to sit down:
he'd have stayed all day.
(Let's be honest. You
can be crucified just so often;
then you've had it. I mean
you're useless; no good
to God, let alone
to anybody else.) So I said
to him after a while—
well, what's up? What do you want?
And he laughed, stupid,
said he was just passing by
and thought he'd say hello.
Great, I said, hello.
So he left.
And I was so d—ned mad
I couldn't even listen
to the radio. I went
and got some coffee.
The trouble with Christ is
he always comes at the wrong time.[4]

Like a meal when you're homeless, you just never know where your next guest is coming from; all we know is that we are to welcome her as Christ. That is not always easy.

8

STABILITY

Staying Put to Get Somewhere

Earlier I listed the three vows that are common to all Christian monasticism—poverty, obedience, and chastity. But a vow of *stability* is unique to Benedictine monks. It is a commitment to stay with the same community for the rest of one's life. And as I will explain in a bit, it has a vital connection to the other vow unique to Benedictines—*conversatio moralis*. Both vows, together with obedience, are listed in 58.17 of the *Rule* as those taken by the monk when he is received into the community. (In some abbeys a monk can take a long time before professing "final vows," which, so to speak, lock him in. By the way, Benedictines don't join an order—as do Jesuits, for instance; they join a house or community by which they then become associated with the Order of St. Benedict.)

"Perseverance in stability," as Benedict puts it (*RB* 58.9), is much like a marriage vow. Monks and married folks promise to stay with the same people for the rest of their lives, even if they are not always in the same geographical location with each other. (This connection between Benedictine spirituality and married or family life is emphasized in the books by Dolores Lecky and David Robinson listed in the suggestions for further reading.) Just as Benedictine monks might spend two years ministering in an abbey's mission in Guatemala, so a husband and wife might have to live apart for a time because of separate callings or special circumstances that make it logistically difficult to do otherwise.

My wife and I were separated by two thousand miles for a year because God's call took her to a church in Newport Beach, California, while I had to finish contractual obligations teaching in Wheaton, Illinois. (A call from Illinois to southern California has to be carefully discerned. God's will and good climate can be mistaken for each other!) Brief visits separated by three- and four-week intervals of isolation from each other could not have been endured had it not been for the "vow of stability," enabled by God's grace, that we had taken three decades earlier. (I often thought of the monks during that year—and not just with regard to stability!)

The vow of stability operates like a homing device for monks. Not only do monks return to the same community after apostolic work, but the monastery becomes "first family," just as the church must become for the nonmonastic Christian.[1] To quote Father Guy when he described the relationship monks have at Blue Cloud Abbey: "God has placed us in a community of people with whom we would not have chosen to live had it been up to us."[2] In fact, this is something I tell each of my classes at the beginning of the semester: I am just enough of a Calvinist to believe that God has called together this *particular* constellation of people to speak to and hear from each other what is needed for their mutual growth in Christlikeness. As Basil is supposed to have said, "God the Creator has arranged things so that we need each other." And that, in a sense, is just what stability is all about in the monastic community.

But it means more than just remaining in place. Spouses, parents, workers, neighbors, and others know that we can live or work somewhere for a long time and be with the same people day after day, yet take little interest in what is happening. Stability means being *faithful* where we are—really paying attention to those with whom we live and to what is happening in our common life.

In fact, persevering in stability is really persevering in *listening*. A person stays where God has put her (not in abusive situations, of course) because it is with that group of folks, *speaking the truth in love*, that she will grow *with them* "to maturity, to the measure of the full stature of Christ," as Paul puts it to the Ephesians (4:11–16).

This is so important to remember today. Change is not always bad, but it can leave us untethered, uncentered, disoriented, and confused. To borrow a phrase from Thomas Kelly, we feel like a "committee of selves."[3] In contrast, Henri Nouwen's comment after visiting a Trappist monastery captures the sense of inner peace that stability can bring: "Wherever I am, at home, in a hotel, in a train, plane or airport, I would not feel irritated, restless, and desirous of being somewhere else or doing something else. I would know that here and now is what counts and is important because it is God himself who wants me at this time and in this place."[4]

We, who often are not content with God's global positioning coordinates for our lives, are more like the gyrovagues, the fourth kind of monk Benedict lists in the *Rule*'s first chapter—a kind worse than sarabaites. The term combines Latin for "circle" and Greek for "wander." In other words, these guys were going around in circles. Benedict says that they roam from monastery to monastery, never staying for more than three or four days; he implies that they leave just before being required to join in the tedious manual labor that aids in one's conversion. His description sounds very contemporary: "Always on the move, they never settle down, and are slaves to their own wills and gross appetites" (*RB* 1.11).

Modern-day gyrovagues believe the grass is greener "over there." The grass is greener in another marriage, another church, another house, another job. The trouble is, once we wander over to the other pasture we usually find out the hue is about the same. But it's not just the hue that remains the same; *we* remain the same. Conversion and growth in character happen when we remain, not when we run. This is where the vow of stability links up with the vow of *conversatio moralis* (conversion of life).

The Latin word *conversatio* is literally translated "conversation," and that's the way I learned it when I memorized Bible verses as part of my spiritual formation in our church's boys' club, Sky Pilots. In this Assembly of God church we used the King James Bible, so 1 Peter 1:15 read, "But as he which hath called you is holy, so be ye holy in all manner of conversation." (*Conversatione* is the Latin translation of the Greek *anastrophe* in this verse.) Fortunately, somewhere along the way I had a knowledgeable adult or two who could explain to me that the word *conversation* meant "conduct" or "a way of life," so this was not simply an exhortation to watch my language. (The "colonel" of our Sky Pilots group, however, did chastise me once for saying "darn," which, as he explained to my horror, *really* meant "d—n."

And just so you don't make the same mistakes I made in my youth, I also learned from him that "doggoneit" really means "godd—mit." I suppose this was the beginning of my Christian formation.)

So the vow *conversatio moralis* really refers to a way of life that is dictated by a person's thoughts and actions. In the case of monks, it's the monastic way of life. It is not merely initial repentance or "turning around." That is *conversio. Conversatio* does *begin* with conversion—a familiar concept to Protestants, sometimes associated with dramatic events in a person's life, just as it was in the experience of two monks I have met.

One of these had been searching—a "seeker" in contemporary Protestant megachurch parlance. Inexplicably, he walked into St. Patrick's Cathedral in New York City on an Ash Wednesday, and, just as inexplicably, he converted to Christianity before he left the building. Subsequently, like Augustine after his conversion, he joined the Roman Catholic Church and the monastic way of life at the same time.

Another of these was a contractor who was fairly wealthy but spiritually poor. On his way to a monastery to do some soul-searching, he listened as he drove to a taped meditation on Jesus's encounter with the rich young ruler—the one whom Jesus invited to "sell all you have, give it to the poor, and come follow me." When he arrived, the contractor was just in time for one of the abbey's daily offices. The reading was from Luke 18, and once again, the contractor heard Jesus's invitation. Convinced that God was trying to tell him something, he ended up giving away his possessions and entering the monastery. He summed up his testimony this way: "Once I had everything, but I had nothing; now I have nothing, but I have everything."

These two underwent the *conversio* that many experience who turn to Christ. But conversion must become *conversa-*

tio—a way of life, a daily walk. Sister Irene Nowell of Mount St. Scholastica Monastery described it well as she unpacked the meaning of *conversatio* for oblates and oblate directors at a conference in Atchison, Kansas: it is "the daily willingness to turn and be turned together, the willingness to be a good example, to live every day in humility and wisdom and peace, praying all the while that Christ bring us all together to everlasting life." The Benedictine idea of *conversatio* is of a process, not a one-time event. It's ongoing and daily.

Robert Louis Wilken nicely illustrated this in reference to Gregory the Great's *Life of Benedict*, where Gregory reflects on what it means for Benedict to "live with himself." Gregory took the words to be a reference to Luke 15:17 (in the Prodigal Son story): "How is it, asks Gregory, that a person who is always with himself can be said to have 'come to himself'? The phrase, says Gregory, means 'Search one's soul continuously' and see oneself always in the presence of God and attend to one's life and actions. . . . 'For we understand the words of God more truly when we "search out [ourselves] in them.""[5]

As we've seen, this *conversatio* takes place in the community or tradition in which God has placed us and which we did not create. As Sister Irene said, we turn and are turned "over and over again, by and with all those with whom we interact and in every situation in which we find ourselves." In the Benedictine tradition there is no monastic life without the community. Benedict was part of the cenobitic tradition, which Pachomius, Augustine, and others had developed before him. This tradition held that spiritual formation could occur only in communal living. While solitary life in the desert for eremitic monks had its advantages, it also had its pitfalls—such as encouragement of pride and self-delusion. If monks wanted to develop character traits like obedience, charity, and humility, it was obvious that those traits were best formed in the constant presence of other people. As I've already noted, it's difficult—if not impossible—to obey someone, love others, and be humble when you are the only person around. This is why the *coenobium* (or monastic community) is called a "school for the Lord's service"—a place in which one can learn the skill of living as a disciple of Jesus Christ.

Michael Casey nicely describes how community can work as an agent of change in our lives:

> When God sets about purifying a human being, the process is accomplished in large measure by human agents. This is because the components of our being which block our receptivity to grace are the very blemishes which other people find ugly. The negative reactions of others serve as a mirror in which we can see reflected those deformations of character against which we need to struggle. The pain we experience in being rejected acts as a purge to motivate us to make ourselves more genuinely lovable. Any advance in this direction has the automatic effect of increasing our openness to the action of God. Of course, one who refuses to acquiesce in the truth of others' reactions becomes more deeply entrenched in the bitterness and recrimination and further away from love and God.[6]

Our tendency is to run, not to stay. The problem with the gyrovague is that he does not stay long enough for the mask to slip a bit. Only when we stay in relationships long enough can we be known in such a way that we are confronted with the reality of ourselves and are challenged to convert. As Rowan Williams puts it so well, "The barriers of egoistic fantasy are broken by the sheer brute presence of other persons."[7]

Williams is right to remind us at this point of the early monastic admonition "Stay in your cell and your cell will teach you everything." Or, in contemporary terms, the grass is *not* always greener on the other side. As Anthony Bloom points out, we often live on the basis of external stimuli. Williams would concur and would further remind us that the monastic life is a refusal to make maturity in Christ dependent on the successful search for fresh stimulation: "Without the humiliating and wholly 'unspiritual' experiences of cell-life—the limited routine of trivial tasks, the sheer tedium and loneliness—there would be no way of confronting human nature. It is a discipline to destroy illusions."[8] Our incessant quest for the latest self-help program, the sexiest partner, the newest American idol, the recently "rediscovered" secret that unlocks human potential or ancient wisdom, the most mind-numbing video game, and even the latest best-selling Christian celebrity's guide to the best life you can imagine can divert our attention from the work of God's grace in us. Many issues in our lives could be sorted out if we gave up some control of our environment and allowed God to surprise us by using the contexts and communities in which he has placed us. This is especially true of a culture in which folks go through relationships with about as much frequency as they recycle aluminum cans.

The phrase "Crockpot Christianity" nicely describes Benedictine stability: I stew slowly in one place until I become what God intended. Stability means I don't run away from myself and others as I find them. And I live in the present—unlike a department store in a nearby mall that put out its Halloween decorations in mid-July. Why is it so important to remain steadfast in the space-time coordinates in which God has placed us? Casey explains: "The purpose of the relentless sameness of the monastic round is to create a climate in which hidden aspects of the personality become manifest. External monotony is an invitation to inner change, whereas novelty and constant variety short-circuit the process of going deeper."[9]

We will discover our true selves as we patiently simmer in communities and relationships to which God has called us. And we will find God there as well, because if we cannot find God where we are, we will not find him elsewhere. Except for those extreme or abusive cases, if you haven't seen God in your marriage, in your present employment, in your neighborhood, or in your church fellowship, then chances are you won't see God in your next marriage, job, neighborhood, or church.

In our consumer-driven, church-(s)hopping approach to Christian community we rarely have to suffer the spiritual equivalent of a strip search. As Martin Luther observed, this is why our families are in many respects the closest thing to the monastic *coenobium* that laypeople get to experience. Our spouses, parents, siblings, and children come to know us well. (By the way, Father Guy's statement ["God has placed us in a community of people with whom we would not have chosen to live had it been up to us"] might apply to all these family members except for our spouse; that is, we do not choose our parents, siblings, and children!) We cannot hide—or at least not for long. They remind us that we are not always what or who we think we are. What a wonderful entrée to the conversion of our lives.

The amazing irony is that only through stability—*staying* where God has put us—can we *change*. If the monk's vow of *conversatio* is a promise never to be satisfied with where we are in our relation with God, then the irony is that we must stay in the same community in order *not* to stay in the same relation with God. As John Henry Newman wisely discerned, "In a higher world it is otherwise, but here below to live is to change, and to be perfect is to have changed often."[10]

By the way, you may have wondered if monks ever break the vow of stability. That is, do they ever leave? Do people who take a vow to be married "until death do us part" ever divorce? It happens. It is never what we intend. It is not what we seek. In both circumstances—the monastery and the marriage—it leaves scars.

BALANCE

God in Everything

Given the stereotypes of monasticism, it might come as a surprise to learn that a keystone of Benedictine spirituality is balance. In fact, a Benedictine motto is "Work, study, and pray." Ideally, a monk might spend six hours at work, three in study (*lectio divina*), and four in prayer (the Daily Office). Actually, five activities are rhythmically woven together in chapter 48 of the *Rule*—prayer, work, rest, study, and eating—all to be done in "proper measure because of the faint-hearted" (*RB* 48.9).

As the phrase "proper measure" implies, Benedict prohibited extremes; he wanted no religious heroes or spiritual gold medalists. He tried to require nothing harsh or hard in the *Rule*. To some Eastern monks (and even some Western orders), his moderate requirements in areas such as food, sleep, and drink might sound like weakness and laxity. Indeed, that was precisely the reaction one of my students had; he had become infatuated with Greek Orthodoxy (of an evangelical persuasion) and had a "see, I told you so" attitude when we visited St. George's Orthodox monastery in Israel during a student trip. There was the strict, rigid, unbending ideal community that matched my student's zeal. But it seems to me that Benedict is closer to the evangelical ideal of "moderation in all things except in zeal for Christ." This moderation that takes into account the "faint-hearted"—indeed Benedict's vision of the spiritual life—provides for solid growth but makes allowances for individual expression, the realities of human life, and changing times and seasons. If Benedict's idea of spiritual formation is something like Bill Monroe's recording of the folk gospel song "I'm Workin' on a Building, a Holy Ghost Buildin'," then the building that Benedict had in mind might be most like a modern earthquake-resistant skyscraper: it's solid, but it has a built-in capacity to sway with the tremors.

Such a spiritual existence is far more likely to weather life's unexpected storms than would a rigid, unbending monolith of fundamentalism. There is danger in recklessly pursuing an ideal. Even virtues can become vices when carried to unreasonable and unbending extremes. Sometimes a wise quarterback is forced to call an audible when the backfield shifts.

Here is an example of Benedictine moderation and the discernment required of the abbot—not to mention the humor I noted earlier:

> Everyone has his own gift from God, one this and another that (1 Cor 7:7). It is, therefore, with some uneasiness that we specify the amount of food and drink for others. . . . The superior will determine when local conditions, work or the summer heat indicates the need for a greater amount. He

must, in any case, take great care lest excess or drunkenness creep in. We read that monks should not drink wine at all, but since the monk of our day cannot be convinced of this, let us at least agree to drink moderately, and not to the point of excess, for wine makes even wise men go astray (Sir 19:2). (*RB* 40.1–2, 5–7)

Obviously Benedict saw the wisdom of a balance between body, mind, and soul. Benedict did not tip the scales inordinately on the side of the soul to the neglect of the body. He is aware that the body's needs are inseparably related to the spirit's health. His is a holistic perspective.

The point is that there is no aspect of life that is outside the restoration of creation that God is accomplishing (Rom. 8:18–27). Everything is part of God's gracious regime in the salvation of his people. Benedict's is no disincarnate spirituality. It is aimed at the conversion of the whole person.

The daily rhythm of life in the monastery is a reminder of this. Though monks can be very busy, theirs is not "busyness." There is a balance to the day that maintains proper perspective. We need this to keep us from serving possessions, egos, jobs, and all the other wonderful things that easily become idols that demand our all.

For the Benedictine, this perspective and balance is centered on the *opus Dei* (work of God)—the times of prayer that punctuate the day at certain hours (hence it is referred to as the "liturgy of the hours" or Horarium), with recitation of Psalms at the heart of each communal "prayer meeting." Originally the liturgy of the hours involved eight times of prayer a day (a number derived from Psalm 119, combining the "midnight" rising in verse 62 and the "seven times a day" in verse 164). These prayers are vigils, lauds (meaning "praise"—morning prayer), prime, terce, sext, none (these last four referring to hours of the day), vespers (evening prayer), and compline ("to complete" or "finish" the day). The more strict Cistercians (or Trappists in some cases) maintain these eight offices, getting up at something like 3:30 a.m. to begin the day. Of course, these types also retire at 9:30 p.m. The less rigorous modern-day Benedictines usually observe about four times of prayer a day, typically beginning with lauds around 6:00 a.m. and ending with compline after supper. Still, the times are set: one cannot follow Paul's injunction to pray *all* the time unless one prays at *some* times.

In part, the point of intentionally returning to prayer during the day is to ensure that attending to one's spiritual life is considered as essential as habitual times of eating meals. We don't ordinarily make out a to-do list for the day and add to it "eat lunch." We are fully committed to consuming food at various times during the day. In fact, some advise eating small portions of a balanced diet six times during the day—not quite the monastic eight, but the same idea. In any case, eating the food that makes it possible to do everything else becomes second nature to us. In the same way, stopping to say the Daily Office allows prayer to permeate everything we do. Columba Stewart makes the point succinctly: "Benedict's most fundamental insight in the *Rule* is that we seek God through ordinary means. . . . Benedict would have us structure each day with several exercises of attentiveness to Christ, each a form of listening and responding to God in prayer."[1]

These set times frame the day in a very effective manner. When I have been at the monastery working on a project (such as a study of early monastic writings on the topic of gluttony), the bell for corporate prayer rings, often right in the middle of a bit of research or a good piece of writing. The bell warns me that I have about five minutes to get myself to the choir before the communal prayers begin; though it's tempting to remain at my research or writing, I put down the pencil or close the book and hurry off to the church, for as the *Rule* asserts, "nothing is to be preferred to the Work of God" (*RB* 43.3). (Benedict was so insistent on promptness for the sake of the community that a tardy monk was apparently required to prostrate himself before the abbot—see *RB* 44.1–3—until the abbot gave him permission to get up and find his assigned stall. I've never seen a monk do this today, but then they are not usually late. I *have* threatened my habitually tardy students with the penalty of prostration, but thought better of it.)

The nonmonastic Christian worker can do something of the same sort as the monks when they stop for times of prayer. In fact, one Benedictine monk published a booklet titled *Take Five*, providing a series of five-minute offices to be said at midday by an individual or a small group. The point is this: repeated times of prayer throughout the workday recenter us and remind us what our daily work is all about and what it is for.

At the same time, work reminds us that life is not simply about prayer. This is a perspective Dietrich Bonhoeffer impressed upon his underground seminary—a small monastic-like community—during the Nazi years:

> Praying and working are two different things. Prayer should not be hindered by work, but neither should work be hindered by prayer. Just as it was God's will that man should work six days and rest and make holy day in His presence on the Sabbath, so it is also God's will that every day should be marked for the Christian by both prayer and work. . . . Only where each receives its own specific due will it become clear that both belong inescapably together. Without the burden and labor of the day, prayer is not prayer, and without prayer work is not work.[2]

This balance of prayer and work helps to keep us from various prideful temptations. For instance, the alternating rhythm has a way of curtailing the inclination to use overwork as a means of self-congratulation. All of us have been guilty of responding to someone's litany of her job's demands with the comeback "You think *you* are busy . . ." We create competition where there was no competition, and we ensure our proud dominance. "Taking five" to pray or recite a psalm also defeats our attempts at self-justification as we place more confidence in our work than in God's sustaining grace. In fact, it's significant that the Daily Office begins with the psalmist's words "Lord, come to my assistance; make haste to help me" (Ps. 40:13 in *RB* 18.1). Our work does not justify our existence. The earth will somehow continue to rotate on its axis even without our feverish activity, and God will still be in control.

In this way our daily work can even become a way to know God more deeply. Monotony, boredom, and repetition can teach us that work is not where we find our ultimate significance. It does not fill us. It does not satisfy us. This is why it's important to distinguish work (a "job") from vocation (a "calling"). It's the difference between *doing* laundry and *being* an artist. Vocation (from the Latin *vocatio*, literally meaning a summons or an invitation) has to do with our God-given identity—who we are called to be in Christ. It's possible to lose a job but not our identity. This is an insight the Christian community can contribute to a culture that increasingly encourages people to find their identity in a job that demands a 24/7 preoccupation. Who we *are* is more than the job we *do*.

Putting our work in perspective in this way does not undermine its significance in our life. Benedictines have always known this. Their emphasis on manual labor that is productive enough to provide the monastery with its material necessities also makes it possible for the monks to be charitable toward others while celebrating the dignity of being human. Indeed, in Genesis 1:28 and 2:15, work is not part of the fallen human's cursed existence but integral to the created human's exalted position (ref. Ps. 8:5–8). In fact, sharing in menial tasks is a way of fully sharing in the human community, such as I observed on my early visits to Blue Cloud Abbey, where *everyone* did housecleaning chores on Saturday.

While I was a doctoral student at Princeton Seminary, I worked at a nearby Presbyterian church in order to lower the monthly rent for our church-owned housing. I oversaw the high school youth program; engaged and disengaged the church alarm system each morning and evening; helped set up and take down what was needed for worship services, weddings, and church school; and, most significantly, cleaned the seven bathrooms in preparation for Sunday's crowd. I suppose a doctoral candidate with three M.A.s could have balked, protesting that it was below him to clean these bathrooms every Saturday. I would have been like the recent M.B.A. grad who reminded his employer of his pedigree when asked to sweep the walk. The employer replied, "No problem. I'll show you how to do it."

Strangely, I discovered a sense of dignity and joy in cleaning the johns. I wasn't "tilling the garden," but I was engaged in manual labor that served others. And as Martin Luther King Jr. reminded us in his sermon "The Drum Major Instinct," in God's kingdom *everyone* can be great, because in God's kingdom "greatness" is the accolade given to those who serve the servants (Mark 10:43–45).

Even more profound, because Benedictine spirituality wants no sectors of life to be isolated from God's presence, work becomes a means through which we can know and love

God more deeply. This concern for the saving significance of even the mundane parts of life is subtly taught in the *Rule*'s list of qualifications for the cellarer (the one in charge of material things in the abbey). The qualities listed in chapter 31 of the *Rule* sound amazingly like those prescribed for the abbot in chapter 2. The cellarer must be wise, mature in conduct, temperate, God-fearing, and like a father to the whole community. He is to keep watch over his own soul, and he will be held accountable for the sick, children, guests, and poor in his care. Above all, he must be humble. Even the tools for which the cellarer is responsible are to be treated with as much care as the sacred vessels used in Communion (as are the people who use them)!

I have often thought of this when tempted to bang around and impatiently sling a pot or ladle in the kitchen when preparing a meal for the family. Then I recall chapter 31 of the *Rule*, and I'm reminded that everything—even a tool—is among God's gracious instruments in the salvation of his people.

In the end, Benedict reminds us that *what* you do is not as important as *how, for whom,* and *to what end* you do it. Any task, no matter how trivial, can have great significance. How much we need to hear this today in a culture (which even invades church precincts) that judges the worth of work on the basis of monetary remuneration or celebrity recognition. We may just be surprised at the great banquet feast of the Lamb when we see a third world carpenter or a frail Albanian nun receiving accolades at the head table while the "rich and famous" are applauding from a darkened corner just inside the door.

Before leaving the subject of prayer and work in this chapter, I'd be remiss if I didn't briefly explain an ancient monastic practice that has more recently become popular in wider Christian circles.[3] The practice of *lectio divina*, or "spiritual reading," is part of the monk's daily life as Benedict outlines it in chapter 48. It especially prepares one for community prayer. It is slow, meditative reading. For example, one might begin reading a New Testament epistle until she comes to a particular verse or phrase that captures her attention; she stops, reflects on the passage until her mind begins to wander, and then moves on in the passage until she comes to rest at another phrase.

Though today's monastics may read anything of spiritual value for *lectio*, in Benedict's day it had to do with scripture. And it included memorization, particularly since low light and few books required psalms to be learned by heart for recitation in the community's daily office.

Obviously, *lectio* is not the same thing as reading the Bible through in one year. The One Year Bible has its place, but *lectio* is not "reading by the pound." It is, as Terrence Kardong puts it, to "slow down and plow through the Bible on all fours." It demands that the reader approach the Bible as a pray-er, rather than as a consumer.

Furthermore, *lectio* is reading the Bible not for information but for formation. Irene Nowell likens the study of scripture without prayer and practice to reading a cookbook without ever cooking or eating. In other words, *lectio* is meditating on spiritual readings in order to be changed. That is why it usually involves reading with the mouth, mind, and memory—to help transform the whole person. (In practice, one might read the Bible in a different language or write out a passage in longhand.) The result of such meditative study is what Jean Leclercq's *The Love of Learning and the Desire for God* describes: to be changed by what is learned rather than to storm the gates of knowledge—to form tastes, desires, passions, attitudes, and dispositions. In the end, it is a practice that determines the way one envisions and responds to the world.

IO

TO CHANGE THE WORLD!

Earlier I debunked the myth that monasticism has little if nothing to do with the "real world." Now I need to make a more daring claim: not only can monasticism be a sign of the *real* world, but it can be an agent of God's redemption of the *fallen* world.

Monastic spirituality is a lot like the image of "resident aliens" (borrowing a phrase from Stanley Hauerwas and William Willimon, who wrote a book using it for a title). Due emphasis is to be placed on both words. That is to say, Benedictine monastic spirituality has a lot to do with remaining distinct from the prevailing ethos of the fallen world by residing as a witness to God's *shalom* in the created cosmos.

This is nothing less than God's call to the exilic community in Babylon:

> Thus says the LORD of hosts, the God of Israel, to all the exiles whom I have sent into exile from Jerusalem to Babylon: Build houses and live in them; plant gardens and eat what they produce. . . . But seek the welfare of the city where I have sent you into exile, and pray to the Lord on its behalf, for in its welfare you will find your welfare. . . . For surely I know the plans I have for you, says the LORD, plans for your welfare and not for harm, to give you a future with hope. (Jer. 29:4–5, 7, 11)

We cannot escape the fallen world, but the most effective and transformative witness to the culture is to be the community that Benedict envisioned in the world's midst. To paraphrase the text in Jeremiah, "the monastic community is to seek the world's welfare, for in the world's welfare all of God's people will find their welfare." (Note: This does not mean we find our welfare in a *corpus Christianum*, such as some in the religious right want to establish.) Justin McCann puts this so well: "The civilized world owes no small debt to [Benedict] and to his sons. The ideal for which he lived and the form of life in which he embodied it, remain still, in the [twenty-first] century as in the sixth, an ideal and a life that are of value not only for individual souls but for the common welfare of human society."[1]

The call to Benedictine spirituality is similar to the call embraced by many Christians: to be in the world God created as loyalists to the cause of Christ. It is to avoid being like the sarabaites, who remain faithful to the world in their deeds: "Still loyal to the world by their actions, they clearly lie to God by their tonsure" (*Rule* 1.7). The community of monastics and of those who imbibe Benedictine spirituality is itself a culture or "world"—a common life (*coenobium*) that is shaped by the story of Jesus of Nazareth and by its central act of worship, the Eucharist (which Benedictines celebrate every day). As I've noted before, Benedict calls this world "a school for the Lord's service" (prologue 45). It is a "peculiar people" (1 Peter 2:9 KJV), a new and separate community, a new society. (1 Peter 2:9–10 also calls the church "a holy nation"—presumably the nation that really *is* "under God" and to which we *should* "pledge allegiance.") This collection of Christians exists as a demonstration to the world: "The countercultural witness of monasticism to the essential dignity of every human person expressed in Benedict's deliberate rejection of conventional forms of social ordering, remains one of the most important gifts of monasticism to Church and society."[2] Yet it is not so much a *counter* culture (a phrase with negative connotations) as an *alternative* culture, called to the conversion or transformation of the world that has fallen.[3] The call is to transform the world through the faithfulness of those who live the kind of life Benedict laid out in the *Rule* and according to an eschatological vision—a future with a hope—informed by an understanding of where God is taking history, not where the worldly world wants to take it.[4]

This means that the monastery must become a "hermeneutic of the gospel,"[5] interpreting the gospel by living out an alternative form of life *for the sake of the world* (Jeremiah again). This is what Benedict originally sought with his *Rule*, which, as I have pointed out before, is nothing but a translation of the gospel into instructions whereby the gospel is to be lived out among us.

Ecumenist Lesslie Newbigin called this "the language of testimony"—a language that challenges the world to be accountable to the truth claims of the gospel, God's ongoing story of salvation as revealed in Jesus Christ.[6] For example, given the Benedictine motto of *pax*, we are called to live out the gospel's claim that praying for and blessing our enemies

110

will be more salvific than destroying them as the world's prevailing ethos often dictates. Again, it means that we might elicit responses similar to that of our State Farm Insurance agent's secretary, who surmised that maybe there *are* more Christians "out there" when she heard of our son's honesty in finding the owner of a parked car he had sideswiped; it was a testimony against the world's prevailing ethos.

Because the prevailing ethos so easily co-opts the church, we need monks in our midst to function as a "caution" sign rather than a "yield" sign to guide our relationship with today's culture. Indeed, what Jacques Ellul once warned about communists and fascists could equally apply to contemporaries who want to place the church's faith in liberal democracy or capitalism, in political parties or left and right ideologies:

> They are incapable of making a genuine revolution in our civilization because they accept the essential basis of this civilization, and confine themselves to moving along the line of its internal development. Thus, utilizing what this world offers them, they become its slaves, although they think that they are transforming it. All the revolutions, advocated both by communism and fascism, are superficial modifications, which change nothing in the real problems of our day.[7]

Ellul's criticism was echoed more recently in Argentine evangelist René Padilla's observations of the North American church: "Far from being a factor for the transformation of society, it has become merely another reflection of society and (what is worse) another instrument that society uses to condition people to its materialistic values."[8]

Monks do get co-opted by marketers of nun dolls, CDs filled with chants, noisy cereal, and quaint greeting cards. But hopefully the ruled vision of life by which their communities are governed will not be so easily corrupted by some of the reigning values of our culture.

As Hauerwas and Willimon put it, "Christian ethics arise, in great part, out of something Christians claim to have seen that the world has not seen, namely, the creation of a people, a family, a colony [and, let us add, a Benedictine monastic community] that is a living witness that Jesus Christ is Lord."[9] Benedictines and Protestants—particularly of an evangelical persuasion—would both say "Amen!" to this.

You can almost hear the concern of some Christians like Padilla in the assessment of our situation made by moral philosopher Alaisdair MacIntyre:

> A crucial turning point in . . . history occurred when men and women of good will turned aside from the task of shoring up the Roman imperium and ceased to identify the continuation of civility and moral community with the maintenance of that imperium. What they set themselves to achieve instead—often not recognizing fully what they were doing—was the construction of new forms of community within which the moral life could be sustained so that both morality and civility might survive the coming ages of barbarism and darkness. . . . We ought to conclude that for some time now we too have reached that turning point. What matters at this stage is the construction of local forms of community within which civility and the intellectual and moral life can be sustained through the new dark ages which are already upon us. And if the tradition of the virtues was able to survive the horrors of the last dark ages, we are not entirely without grounds for hope. This time however the barbarians are not waiting beyond the frontiers; they have already been governing us for quite some time. And it is our lack of consciousness of this that constitutes part of our predicament. We are waiting not for a Godot, but for another—doubtless very different—St. Benedict.[10]

This is the Benedict who gave us instruction in virtues like obedience, stability, and balance in life. We would all do well to listen once again and appropriate what this saint offered the undivided Christian world a millennium and a half ago.

Every day Benedictine monastics pray, "Animate us with the Spirit with which Benedict was animated." This is the Spirit of Jesus Christ—the Spirit who animates Protestants, Roman Catholics, and Orthodox alike—and this is the *only* animating Spirit by whom Benedictine-inflected Christians will continue to survive in a world that desperately needs to see their witness.

A Historical Afterword

*Why the Protestant Reformers
Opposed Monasticism*

The fact that monasticism is relatively foreign to Protestants leads to misunderstandings of a general nature on both sides of the wall. (There are a few Protestant monastic groups, such as the Episcopal Society of St. John the Evangelist and the Episcopal Benedictine house in Three Rivers, Michigan.) Once, when I was saving curbside seats for the Disney Light Parade, I struck up a conversation with a female adherent of a monastic order (not Benedictine) and mentioned to her that I was an oblate of a Benedictine house. When further discussion revealed that I was a Presbyterian, she was stunned and said, "I didn't know that we were that liberal!"

On the other hand, I have Protestant acquaintances who are convinced that Catholics worship Mary and resacrifice Jesus every time Mass is said. For better understanding of each other, sometimes it's good to do a bit of research to get our facts straight, such as consulting the Catechism of the Catholic Church or poking around in sixteenth-century church history. At least we'll be better prepared for pleasant conversation at the great banquet feast of the Lamb.

For reasons that will be made clear, those in the Augustinian tradition (including Roman Catholics) have often been suspicious of the theology underlying Benedictine monasticism—that of John Cassian. Add to that the Protestant Reformers' disdain of much late medieval monasticism in the Catholic Church, and it seems that there is a high hurdle to jump if one is going to successfully recommend monasticism to Protestants.

Cassian's theology lies behind much of Benedict's thinking (which is why he commends Cassian's works to the *Rule*'s reader in *RB* 73.5). But Cassian was usually suspect in the West because of his alleged "semi-Pelagianism," a charge leveled against him by one of Augustine's disciples. For instance, in *The Conferences* 13.8.4, Casssian wrote: "When he [God] notices good will making an appearance in us, at once he enlightens and encourages it and spurs it on to salvation, giving increase to what he himself planted and saw arise from our own efforts."[1] It sounded as if Cassian was throwing in his hat with Pelagius, holding that we all have an innately good will to which God responds with his grace, lending aid to a capacity that has not been inherently diminished by the sin of our first parents.

But Cassian scholars such as Owen Chadwick[2] and Columba Stewart[3] argue that Cassian rejected the extremes of both Pelagius and Augustine—that he simultaneously stressed our absolute dependence on God's grace *and* the full responsibility of humans with their free will to choose between good and evil. This is illustrated in his simile of the farmer (*Conferences* 13.3): crops will not grow unless the farmer toils, but, equally, crops will not grow unless there is sufficient sunshine and rain. Cassian was not interested in metaphysical speculation or the niceties of doctrinal theories of grace and free will (as was Augustine in his dispute with Pelagius) but in the lived experience of the monk in the monastic tradition. Cassian's interests reflected more of the Eastern emphasis on practical and moral consequences: "he writes as a participant in a process of spiritual growth that is a mysterious interplay of human and divine elements."[4] As a result, Cassian pits grace not against free will but against laziness or torpor.

Thus Cassian was not a Pelagian, since he emphasized the paramount necessity of the interior working of God's grace for salvation from start to finish. This ascetical theologian was preaching to the choir, assuming the prevenience and concomitance of grace all the way and stressing the responsibility of our will to work against sloth. He did not believe that total reliance on spiritual disciplines would save us (any more than the farmer would be wise to calculate the success of a harvest on his efforts alone), that such work would bring us to perfection, or that God dispenses his grace as a reward based on some merit that our disciplined life has earned. But he did believe that monastic-type disciplines, offered in the right spirit, could provide God an opportunity to confer the divine grace needed to complete our human efforts.

At the same time, Cassian was not Augustinian either, for he was concerned that convictions about predestination and irresistible grace could encourage lukewarmness or halfheartedness. Unlike Augustine, Cassian believed that the fall had not reduced humans to an incapacity to do good but had weakened the will so that there is always a tension between the innate inclination of sinful passions and the pull of spiritual desires.[5] Cassian believed that we can see this seemingly unpredictable interplay of grace and human will in scripture itself. But since he does no more than simply juxtapose the two, to some in the West he seems inconsistent and open to the charge of Pelagianism. As a result, Cassian was not given saint's status in the West but was venerated in the East (albeit with a feast day on February 29—i.e., only in leap years). Perhaps a failure to understand the subtleties I have noted contributed to the Protestant Reformers' rather strident rejection of monasticism.

Michael Casey seems to caution us against this oversight when he discusses the fact that in the *Rule* Benedict demonstrates a high estimation of the importance of grace. Casey surmises that this may have been motivated by efforts at self-protection from the charges that had been laid out against Cassian:

> Because monastic life demands effort, it sometimes happens that monastic authors seem to place too much emphasis on the human contribution to growth in godliness. Many of their writings are directed to inciting the will to make a choice to live well. Grace was taken for granted. The rectitude and effectiveness of the human power of decision seemed more in need of encouragement and support. There is much moral exhortation in monastic texts, but it was never intended to be read outside the context of the inspiration and energy of grace. When we read texts like the *Rule of Benedict* we need to keep reminding ourselves of their implicit theology of grace.[6]

Of course, by the time we get to the Protestant Reformation, Benedictine monasticism had undergone a millennium of changes, joined along the way by other monastic movements, each with its own characteristics. No wonder that there was not a consensus about monasticism even among late medieval theologians in the "pre-Reformed" church.

(Actually, criticisms of monasticism even go back to the ancient church.) Some like Thomas Aquinas argued that works performed on the basis of monastic vows were more meritorious, while others like John Pupper of Goch severely criticized Thomas's views of the religious life, anticipating the Protestant Reformers' arguments and arguing that there was no warrant in the New Testament for a vowed life that was incompatible with Christian freedom and that vows do not increase merit.[7] The variety of opinions, along with the social significance and commoners' perceptions of the religious orders, is the backdrop for a brief look at what bothered Ulrich Zwingli, Martin Luther, John Calvin, and other Protestants who reacted to sixteenth-century monasticism.[8]

Beyond mere iconoclasm, the reasons that Protestant Reformers did not look kindly on monasticism generally fall under three rubrics. First, they argued that it was inherently schismatic, setting up a two-tiered system of Christian commitment and lifestyle—a system that distinguished precepts, by which all Christians are to live who aspire to eternal life, and "counsels of perfection" (such as commitments to poverty and celibacy) that will lead one toward perfection. Second, they had a slew of objections to monastic vows, the most significant of which had to do with Protestant concerns over the basis for justification. And third, they complained that monks were prone to "idleness"—that is, they were kept from fulfilling the duties of Christian ministry by the very nature of their commitments (an ironic charge, given Cassian's concern to counter laziness).

Calvin's principal objection to monasticism was what he saw as its inherently and unavoidably schismatic character. Understanding the monastic vows as a "second baptism," Calvin argued that monasticism lacks biblical support and establishes a "double Christianity" that separates monks from the whole body of the church. David Steinmetz insists, "Whatever other faults monasticism might have had in Calvin's eyes, this fault alone was sufficient to condemn it."[9] Zwingli, Luther, and Calvin all agreed that the separation of "counsels of perfection" for monks (such as Jesus's instructions in the Sermon on the Mount) from "precepts" (such as the Ten Commandments) for all other Christians, who must be satisfied with imperfection and second-class status, was not only schismatic but misguided. What one vowed at baptism is what God expects of all disciples. In fact, Zwingli argued that making a vow of doing what God already commands is really insubordinate: "Why, then, do they make a vow of the law itself, as if they could keep it better having vowed than by obeying the commandment of God? . . .What is the use of vowing poverty? The Christian heart is not Christian unless it is poor. . . . According to the law [Matt. 5:3], therefore, we ought all to be poor; and those who are not fail to obey the law."[10] In other words, the Sermon on the Mount is not a series of optional "counsels" but commandments for all Christians.

Benedictine monastics today would deplore such a division of divine expectations and Christian caste system. In fact, they just might be the first to admit they fall far short of many Christians who live daily lives in the secular arena.

It's to be hoped that Luther would be a bit more circumspect in his condemnation of monasticism if he were around Benedictines today. At one point he characteristically lashed out, "To become a monk (unless one is saved by a miracle) is to become an apostate from faith, to deny Christ, and to become a Jew, and, as Peter prophesied, to return to one's heathen vomit."[11] A bit later he outdid himself when he suggested that vows, apart from faith, are "ungodly, heathen, Jewish, sacrilegious, lying, erroneous, satanic, hypocritical,

apostate, and even contrary to the examples of the saints."[12]
It was this that bothered Luther the most. If schism was
Calvin's primary concern regarding monasticism, Luther was
primarily concerned with the vows that many swore but few
kept, not so much because monks did not keep them in his
opinion but primarily because the whole notion struck at
the heart of Luther's soteriology (or theology of salvation):
"For they teach justification and salvation by works, and
depart from faith. They not only think that their obedience,
poverty, and chastity are certain roads to salvation, but that
their ways are more perfect and better than those of the rest
of the faithful. This is an open, obvious lie, and an error and
sin against faith. All they have is hypocrisy and a branded
conscience."[13]

Luther believed that monastic vows smacked of justification by works of the law and were therefore a denial of
salvation through Christ. He wrote, "No man shall live by
his works, and, by the same token, no man shall live by his
vows."[14] It is no wonder that Luther reacted so violently
against the institution to which he had earlier committed
himself when a member of the Augustinian order. For Luther, taking and keeping monastic vows had nothing to do
with faith; they were "some kind of law" by which the
monk sought to earn his salvation, obtain grace, and wipe
away his sins.[15] They struck at the heart of the Reformer's
understanding of justification.

As a result, Luther believed that apart from faith monastic
vows were unacceptable and worthless in God's sight and
that all monks should be absolved of their vows. In fact, he
insisted that God will be as merciful to us for breaking any
vow except those of obedience to parents and love of neighbor as he is toward those who break his law, especially since,
in the case of celibacy, breaking the vow in order to marry

is to avoid sinning worse against God's law.[16] As Luther put it, "Nothing that is contrary to love, and nothing more than love, is or can be binding."[17]

Today's Benedictines take their vows seriously, but just as they would not rate their Christian profession any higher than the secular Christian's, so they would share Luther's conviction that God forgives the one who breaks his vow in order to marry rather than "burn" (1 Cor. 7:9). I know this because, just as Samuel Johnson remarked when he was asked if he believed in infant baptism, "Believe it? I've seen it done!" I remember in particular one monk from Blue Cloud Abbey who, after years in the monastery, married a woman in the nearby town. The step was not taken lightly by any means, but it was also not taken without grace.

There were other reasons that the Protestant Reformers held vows in contempt. Both Luther and Calvin believed vows contradicted Christian freedom. Luther insisted that the Christian is to be free from all in order to be free for all. And Calvin put it succinctly when he wrote:

> Here it is, then, in a nutshell. God has made us lords of all things and has so subjected them to us that we may use them all for our own benefit. Consequently, if we yield ourselves in bondage to external things (which ought to be a help to us), there is no reason why we should expect it to be a service acceptable to God. I say this because some try to win praise for humility through ensnaring themselves in many observances, from which God has with good reason willed us to be free and exempt.[18]

Of course, Protestants, particularly of the fundamentalist variety, cannot exactly say that Calvin's admonition does not apply to them. Once, when I was a faculty member at a Protestant college that proscribed the use of alcohol and dancing 24/7, twelve months a year, I attended a banquet at a Benedictine conference where bottles of wine were set at each table. The sister who sat next to me asked if I'd like a glass of wine. Truthfully I had to answer that I would *like* a glass but I couldn't *have* a glass. She looked a bit puzzled, so I tried to explain: "I teach at a college where I took something like a vow to abstain from drinking alcohol." Then I couldn't resist adding, "But I prefer to give up what I gave up rather than what you gave up." With good reason that sister didn't say much to me at the banquet; I deserved the cold shoulder.

Calvin's point rings true nonetheless: "If we yield ourselves in bondage to external things (which ought to be a help to us), there is no reason why we should expect it to be a service acceptable to God." Indeed, an evangelical from England (God bless British evangelicals!) was appalled to learn the college's rules regarding the consumption of wine, and I was equally surprised when he stated his reason: "I think it's a matter of discipleship to the Lord Jesus Christ." I think he'd read Calvin.

The vow of celibacy (the one that the sister took and I did not!) particularly bothered the Reformers as being against human nature. Zwingli, for one, insisted that continence is God's gift and one should not pledge what is not in his power to pledge. Arguing from 1 Corinthians 7, Zwingli left it up to the individual to decide how the passion burns, but "if your mind reel at the mention of Venus" you had best not seek celibacy.[19] Calvin agreed: we should only take a vow of celibacy according to "that measure which God by his gift sets" for us; otherwise we "strive" against the nature given to us, demean marriage, and act arrogantly and with contempt of God's gifts due to overconfidence.[20] And Luther made the point in his characteristically graphic manner:

"Imagine, I beg you, a madman who vowed something like this to God, 'I vow to thee, O Lord, to make new stars or to move mountains.' What would you think of such a vow? Yet the vow of chastity is no different from a vow like that, for chastity is no less wonderful a work of God than creating stars and moving mountains."[21]

Luther tended to use *chastity* and *celibacy* interchangeably. And indeed, for Christians they do belong together when one is unmarried. It's significant, then, that Stewart argues that the centerpiece of Cassian's theology is the concept of chastity, for it is an abiding tranquillity of the passions that involves the entire person—body and spirit—at all times; therefore, it is beyond the reaches of the human will. Chastity is the basis for human relationships founded truly on love, over against selfish desire or vainglorious manipulation. And while the Reformers were right that celibacy must be a gift of God, Stewart makes it clear that Cassian would insist with them that *chastity* can only be a gift of God. (See his *Conferences* 13.4.6.) As Stewart puts it so well, "Sheer determination might battle sexual desire to a truce but can never produce the inner purification effected by grace."[22] That is, while Cassian aligned himself with Augustine on the central fact of dependence on God's grace, his theology of grace took ascetical efforts (i.e., spiritual disciplines) seriously, while avoiding the errant extreme of complete reliance on these disciplines. In fact, it is precisely one's experience with the limitations of ascetical disciplines—of sheer willpower—that leads one to realize that purity cannot be achieved through human effort but ultimately only by God's grace. This is why Cassian has a chapter in the *Conferences* on "nocturnal emissions" or "wet dreams." (The Victorian translation of Cassian's work in the *Nicene and Post-Nicene Fathers* did not include this chapter or the one on chastity! It took twentieth-century Benedictine monks to get them into English!) His point was that while one *might* be able to maintain chaste thoughts when awake, nighttime thoughts are unguarded; only by God's grace can even our dreams be chaste. The point of this discussion is that a Benedictine like Columba Stewart would go a long way today to argue *with* the Reformers that vows can be taken and kept only by God's gifting.

Though the Reformers often criticized monks for hypocrisy and cultivating the opposite of vowed virtues (a charge that has had truth behind it at certain points in monastic history), they did recognize the benefits of vows under certain conditions. If vows connected with religious life are not employed as a means of justification, if they are not permanently binding, and if they do not go against or beyond what Christ commanded, Luther thought that one might use them as means to discipline the body to better serve one's neighbor and meditate on God's Word. You might do this just as another person might take up farming or a trade, "without any thoughts of merits or justification."[23] Luther nicely summarizes his position here as he considers Romans 14:2–3 and 1 Corinthians 7:18–19:

> And so, if you vow to take up the religious life, and if you live with men of like mind, with a clear conscience that in monasticism you seek nothing to your advantage in your relationship with God, but because either your situation has brought you to embrace this kind of life, or it appeared to be the best way of life for you, without your thinking thereby that you are better than he who takes up a wife or takes up farming, then in that case you are neither wrong to take vows nor wrong to live in this way, insofar as the propriety of the vow is concerned. But if love should demand that the vow be broken and you were to hold fast to your vow, you would be sinning.[24]

Calvin concurred with Luther on these stipulations for taking appropriate vows. More specifically, the intentions of one who took monastic vows might include expressions of gratitude or repentance or efforts to arouse us to a concern or to some duty; but in any case, such vows must be approved by God, agree with one's calling, and be limited to the grace that God has given the individual.[25]

Beyond these arguments against monastic vows and a schismatic two-tiered Christianity, the Protestant Reformers also charged monks with "idleness." That is, they believed that the promises monastics made kept them from fulfilling Christian responsibilities and ministries in the world.

Calvin was not impressed by the ordination of cloistered monks in the late Middle Ages. He insisted that these were mutually exclusive: one was ordained to the service of the Word and sacraments, while the other was called to withdraw from the world for contemplative prayer. In the end, Calvin considered the former and any service of obedient love in society a higher calling than the latter.[26]

This also involved the vows monks took. For instance, Calvin recognized the beauty in abandoning one's possessions to follow Christ, but he believed that it was an even more lovely act to rule one's household in the fear of the Lord. The story of the rich young ruler had to be read in the context of 1 Corinthians 13:

> It was a beautiful thing to forsake all their possessions and be without earthly care. But God prefers devoted care in ruling a household, where the devout householder, clear and free of all greed, ambition, and other lusts of the flesh, keeps before him the purpose of serving God in a definite calling. . . . Though we grant that there was nothing evil in that profession, it was surely no slight evil that it brought a useless and dangerous example into the church.[27]

126

Zwingli echoed Calvin's sentiments; he not only accused the monks of merely pretending poverty but charged these avowed rich of not sharing the cares of wealth nor the burdens of the government by paying taxes. And Zwingli had similar criticisms of the vow of celibacy. He argued that it dishonors marriage and the family, deprives the state of useful citizens, and disregards God's mandate that parents have and rear children.[28]

These same criticisms are heard today as well. In fact, it may be surprising to read a similar complaint made by a contemporary Cistercian monk. Michael Casey writes:

> The fact that Matthew's picture of the Final Judgment does not inspire a certain uneasiness in monks and nuns must give us pause. How is it that we who profess to pursue an evangelical life exclude from our normal lifestyle the very activities on which Christians will be assessed? Most of us are not personally involved in feeding the hungry, clothing the naked, or visiting jails. By what means do we rationalize such massive omission? Staying at home, keeping silence, and following orders are scarcely substitutes for objective conformity with the teaching of Christ. You would think that monastics might have the decency sometimes to feel a little disturbed at the ambiguity of their profession.[29]

To be fair, Casey might be more zealous in his criticism than he needs to be (though he is speaking as a member of the stricter order coming out of the Benedictine tradition—the Cistercians). For one thing, many modern-day monastics are involved in meeting the needs of the dispossessed, the marginalized, and the impoverished. The monks of Blue Cloud Abbey, for instance, settled in South Dakota to minister to Native Americans in the Dakotas. They established churches and schools, and they housed a museum of cultural artifacts and reference materials (with Fr. Stan, who is now deceased, acting as the very knowledgeable curator). They also established a monastery in Guatemala; from there they brought back beautiful woven cloth out of which Br. Sebastian made paraments (altar cloths and vestments) that found their way into most of the Roman Catholic parishes in the Dakotas (and also into my closet), the proceeds from which were shared with the Guatemalan weavers. Benedictine monks have supported the arts, administered successful inner-city schools, run hospitals, cared for the elderly—and the list goes on. So while Casey's evaluation may call modern monastics to do even more, it is not the case that they are as out of touch as common misperceptions would have it or as the Protestant Reformers considered their own contemporaries to be.

At the same time, when one points a finger, three are pointing back. We have only to substitute "confessing Protestants" for "monks and nuns" and "monastics" in Casey's quote and we have to admit we are guilty as charged. It may not be permanent vows that keep us from attending to our Christian responsibilities; it may be grown-up toys, workaholism, or simply a case of apathy.

So is monasticism salvageable for Protestants? The Reformers actually thought so, to a degree. Calvin and Luther both praised the early founders of religious orders—especially folks like Antony (credited with being the first eremitic monk), Augustine, and Francis. Luther compared the late medieval situation to the time of the children of Israel who did not know "God's works and marvelous deeds" as the patriarchs did. Instead, he said, they fretted over rules, laws, and customs, "without ever reaching a true understanding of what constitutes a religious and virtuous life." The antidote, suggests Luther, is for monasteries and priories to return to the way they were once regulated, when they functioned as Christian schools to teach scripture, Christian morals, church leadership, homiletics, and the like to "students" (particularly young people) who were under no constraint of vows.[30]

Calvin echoes Luther's praise for a "moderate monasticism"—the kind that Augustine described in *On the Morals of the Catholic Church*.[31] Here Calvin also suggests that early monasteries played the role of "monastic colleges" or "seminaries of the ecclesiastical order" in which "pious men customarily prepared themselves by monastic discipline to govern the church, that thus they might be fitter and better trained to undertake so great an office"; they constituted a "community in aid of piety, whose rule was tempered by the goal of brotherly love."[32] Thus Calvin suggests, as Luther did, that Augustine's description of early monastic practice should function as the norm by which to judge defects in the monasticism of his day.

In reality, this is precisely the directive of Vatican Council II when it admonished monastic orders in the document *Perfectae Caritatis* to rediscover their foundings and charisms. Benedictine monastics have taken this seriously, and today the abbeys that dot the landscape often live up to Benedict's ideal as "schools for the Lord's service." Zwingli, Luther, and Calvin might have been impressed—maybe.

Suggested Reading

The list that follows is not intended to be an exhaustive bibliography. There are several reasons for my choices here. First, some of these books are my favorites. Second, the variety of authors will introduce you to, well, a variety of authors. Third, this list provides a sampling of different categories of books on Benedictine monasticism (which may just get you going in a direction you'd like to go). Some folks familiar with Benedictine monasticism will be upset that their favorite is not listed. I would be too if I were they.

For those who want to study the *Rule of St. Benedict*, there are many editions of the rule and many commentaries. The most commonly used translation of the *Rule* with wonderful notes and essays on various topics is Timothy Fry, OSB, ed., *RB1980: The Rule of St. Benedict in Latin and English with Notes* (Collegeville, MN: Liturgical Press, 1981). I'm willing to lend my books to others, but this is one I don't let out of my sight, since it represents an invaluable compendium of information about Christian monasticism. A "lite" version of this is the more recent *The Benedictine Handbook* (Collegeville, MN: Liturgical Press, 2003). The most definitive (verse by verse) commentary on the *Rule of Benedict* is an amazing work (with an equally amazing price!): Terrrence G. Kardong, OSB, *Benedict's Rule: A Translation and Commentary* (Collegeville, MN: Liturgical Press, 1996). The extent of Kardong's knowledge astounds me.

For those who want to study the history and character of Benedictine monasticism, Kardong is again helpful with his book *The Benedictines* (Wilmington, DE: Michael Glazier, 1988). And if one wants to study the theological origins of Benedictine spirituality, one place to go to is Columba Stewart, OSB, *Cassian the Monk* (New York: Oxford University Press, 1998). For scholars it's an impressive piece, about a third of which is footnotes, but for those who are not so scholarly it's an equally impressive piece because it reads so well. These studies might lead a person to go to the sources themselves, reading Cassian's *Conferences* or *Institutes* or (a century earlier) Evagrius Ponticus's *Praktikos* or (a century later) Gregory the Great's *Pastoral Care* (which is one of the best things that has ever been written on pastoral counseling).

For those who want to know what the life of monks is really like, no book may be better than my oblate director's account of his own life and the often comical lives of his fellow monks at Blue Cloud Abbey: Benet Tvedten, OSB, *The View from a Monastery* (Brewster, MA: Paraclete, 2006). An outsider's view of the inside is described well by Frank Bianco, *Voices of Silence: Lives of Trappists Today* (New York: Anchor, 1991); the unfolding story of Fr. Bede has an amazing finish.

For those who would like to read what Benedictine monastics have to say about their own tradition of spirituality, it's hard to beat the wordsmith Joan Chittister, OSB, *Wisdom*

Distilled from the Daily: Living the Rule of St. Benedict Today (San Francisco: Harper and Row, 1990). Another interesting book along these lines combines introductory reflective essays on various topics by a scholar in his own right, each followed by a few pages of choice quotes from a variety of sources: Hugh Feiss, OSB, ed., *Essential Monastic Wisdom: Writings on the Contemplative Life* (San Francisco: HarperSanFrancisco, 1999). And if one wants to go hard core, go for Charles Cummings, OCSO, *Monastic Practices* (Kalamazoo, MI: Cistercian Publications, 1986), and Michael Casey, OCS, *A Guide to Living in the Truth: Saint Benedict's Teaching on Humility* (Ligouri, MO: Ligouri/Triumph, 2001).

For those who want to learn more about Benedictine oblates, a good introduction is Benet Tvedten, OSB, *How to Be a Monastic and Not Leave Your Day Job: An Invitation to Oblate Life* (Brewster, MA: Paraclete, 2006). A collection of essays provides a survey of the lives of some oblates, some well known and some not so well known: Linda Kulzer, OSB, and Roberta Bondi, eds., *Benedict in the World: Portraits of Monastic Oblates* (Collegeville, MN: Liturgical Press, 2002).

Those who want to read what oblates themselves have written about Benedictine spirituality could start with the most well known of the bunch, whose books have been on the top of the *New York Times* bestseller list: Kathleen Norris, *Dakota: A Spiritual Geography* (New York: Ticknor and Fields, 1993), and *The Cloister Walk* (New York: Riverhead, 1996). Norris has since written several more books and forewords to some of the others mentioned throughout this list. *Dakota* is a beautiful book that brings together small-town Dakota life and the monastery in a prose that is poetic. *Cloister Walk* is really a collection of essays Norris wrote during two extended visits to St. John's Abbey in Collegeville, Minnesota. She's a Presbyterian, as is another oblate author, Eric Dean, *Saint Benedict for the Laity* (Collegeville, MN: Liturgical Press, 1989). Others (of the Anglican tradition) include Esther de-Waal, *Seeking God: The Way of St. Benedict*, 2nd ed. (Collegeville, MN: Liturgical Press, 2001), and Brian C. Taylor, *Spirituality for Everyday Living: An Adaptation of the Rule of St. Benedict* (Collegeville, MN: Liturgical Press, 1989). deWaal's book was one of the first of these kinds of books by a nonmonastic, and it's become something of a classic. Taylor's is very brief (seventy pages) but packed with insights, and it's great as a study guide for small groups.

One of the first to explore the application of Benedictine spirituality to family life was Dolores R. Leckey, *The Ordinary Way: A Family Spirituality* (New York: Crossroad, 1987). More recently, a Presbyterian pastor has investigated how the family can function as a kind of monastery: David Robinson, *The Family Cloister: Benedictine Wisdom for the Home* (New York: Crossroad, 2000). An oblate of St. Andrew's Abbey in Valyermo, California (where they have a huge arts festival every September), who has written several books on Benedictine spirituality, reflects on the application of the *Rule* to the way lay folks think about their work: Norvene Vest, *Friend of the Soul: A Benedictine Spirituality of Work* (Boston: Cowley, 1997).

Finally, for those who want to say the Daily Office, there are several books available, including *The Benedictine Handbook* (Collegeville, MN: Liturgical Press, 2003); *Shorter Morning and Evening Prayer* (Collegeville, MN: Liturgical Press, 1987); *Saint Benedict's Prayer Book for Beginners* (York, UK: Ampleforth Abbey Press, 1993); and *Take Five: Prayers for the Workplace* (Collegeville, MN: Liturgical Press, 1989).

SUGGESTIONS FOR PRACTICING BENEDICTINE SPIRITUALITY

Dallas Benedictine Experience, June 23–27, 2004—Fifteen suggestions for developing a personal rule of life in response to "How to Take Benedictine Spirituality Home with You":

1. Pray at least two Offices daily.
2. Read and meditate on sacred scripture at least once a day.
3. Practice times of silence.
4. Practice a contemplative type of prayer daily.
5. Remember that every moment of our lives is lived in the Divine Presence.
6. Do a partial or full fast (or abstain from meat) at least once a week.
7. Attend church services and/or receive the Holy Eucharist at least once weekly.
8. Care for those you live with, work with, and worship with.

9. Treat your family and your daily work/profession as your main Christian ministry.
10. Refrain from judging others and pray for them instead.
11. Be consistently involved in at least one ministry/program of your parish.
12. Treat all physical objects in your environment with care and reverence.
13. Remember *RB* 4: "The love of Christ must come before all else."
14. Be faithful (stable) in your family, employment, parish responsibilities.
15. Serve others with consistent patience and care.

Oblate Directors' Guidelines, June 1973:

Oblates strive to be loyal and active members of Christ and his Church

. . . for their own continued Christian renewal and personal improvement.

. . . to be men and women of practical spirituality.

. . . to be men and women of prayer.

. . . to be men and women of Christian virtue.

Oblates foster a spirit of community.
Oblates are men and women of peace.

NOTES

Chapter 1 What's a Good (Protestant Evangelical) Boy Doin' in a Monastery?

1. Originally, oblates were children who were "offered"—as the etymology of the word implies—to monasteries, usually with a gift of money as well, to be religiously trained and educated during the Middle Ages. Though this sounds terrible to modern ears, it was a win-win situation: many times parents could not feed another child in their large family, the child would receive a literary education that was not otherwise available to most children, and the monastery could sustain its community. (See the *Rule*, chapter 59.) Today an oblate is someone who wants to practice what Benedict taught in his or her daily life, daily seeking God in the "Benedictine way," including spiritual reading (particularly of scripture), prayer, and work. The oblate associates with a particular Benedictine community. But the oblate lives and works in the world, applying the teachings and principles of the *Rule of St. Benedict* to his or her own life circumstances, and thereby witnesses to the world of Christ, bringing the gospel message and God's way of holiness to the world (particularly since the *Rule of Benedict* is simply the application of Jesus's teachings to everyday living). An oblate director keeps in touch and instructs oblates through letters and meetings. Oblates do not take on any of the canonical obligations that monks and nuns do. They do not profess vows. But one becomes an oblate after serious consideration, usually after a year "novitiate." Finally, the *Oblate Directors' Guidelines* (1973) states, "Since Oblates of St. Benedict primarily offer themselves for the service of God and others, they will therefore strive for God's honor and glory before all else, keeping in mind the Benedictine motto: 'That in all things God may be glorified'" (*RB* 57, quoting 1 Peter 4:11). An excellent introduction to the whole business of Benedictine oblation is the book *How to Be a Monastic and Not Leave Your Day Job* by Benet Tvedten, OSB (Brewster, MA: Paraclete, 2006). Br. Benet just happens to be my oblate director, and a very

136

good one. As Benet mentions (on p. 70), some prominent recent oblates have been Dorothy Day, Jacques and Raissa Maritain, Sir Alec Guinness, Walker Percy, Senator Eugene McCarthy, and Rose Kennedy (JFK's mother). Benet states there are an estimated 24,155 Oblates of St. Benedict today (p. 109).

"The American Benedictine Academy is a non-profit association whose purpose is to cultivate, support and transmit the Benedictine heritage within contemporary culture. The Academy sponsors and promotes disciplinary and inter-disciplinary research, writing and collaboration among its members. It serves as a catalyst inviting men and women to ponder creatively and to discuss the challenges to Benedictine values in the twenty-first century" (from the ABA website). The academy fulfills these goals through the activities and publications, especially a biennial convention that focuses on a theme relevant to the Benedictine heritage (these are held at monastic institutions around the United States and are open to any interested persons) and a quarterly publication, *The American Monastic Newsletter*.

2. See the afterword for accounts of the Protestant Reformers' objections to monasticism and why Cassian (an early-fifth-century monk) was not appreciated in the Western Church.

Chapter 2 Why Benedictine Spirituality for Protestants?

1. Richard Foster, *Celebration of Discipline*, rev. ed. (San Francisco: Harper and Row, 1988), 1.

2. Dietrich Bonhoeffer, *Cost of Discipleship*, trans. R. H. Fuller, with some revision by Irmgard Booth (orig. 1959; New York: Touchstone, 1995), 46.

3. Benedict was born in 480 in the mountainous Umbrian province of Nursia to an upper-class family. Early in his life he went to Rome to study the liberal arts, but after a year and a religious conversion, he abandoned his studies and left the city. He spent two years east of Rome with a group of ascetics in a city then called Enfide, where, according to Gregory (his hagiographer), he performed his first miracle. He was probably twenty years old when he went on to Subiaco, where he lived alone for three years on a hillside, being ministered to by a neighboring monk who brought him bread.

As his notoriety grew, he was persuaded by the monks of a monastery (that tradition identifies as Vicavaro), against his better judgment, to come out of solitude to replace their lost abbot. Gregory tells us they tried to poison Benedict's drink after they found his demands too burdensome, but the poison was detected when Benedict blessed what they were about to drink and the pitcher cracked, exposing the plot. Benedict graciously left unharmed and alive.

He returned to Subiaco, where many gathered around him to become his disciples. Eventually he established twelve monasteries, each with twelve monks overseen by a dean and each on a hillside.

As mentioned, he was about fifty years old when he founded the monastery at Monte Cassino, where he spent the rest of his life. He met with his sister Scholastica, a nun, once each year; the last meeting was prolonged by a miraculous thunderstorm, according to Gregory's account, so that this sister could spend more time with her brother shortly before he died.

Gregory's *Dialogues* is the only account we have of Benedict's life, and one has to sift through legend to discern some of the facts. But set alongside the *Rule*, it provides a good stylistic portrait of the man.

4. The word *regula* is translated "rule" and refers to a practical guide for living the Christian gospel and cultivating Christian virtue (ref. *RB* prologue 21). It is like wisdom literature in the Old Testament (*not* like law): it passes on the tradition of wisdom from the lived experience of monastic life—not some abstract rules handed down from lofty atemporal heights.

In the sixth century, a rule served only to regulate the day-to-day life of *one* monastery (fashioned after the Roman codification of Justinian law). Thus, the *Rule of Benedict* was for Monte Cassino. Monasteries often used many rules, taking from each what they found useful for their situations. The *Rule of Benedict* draws on the Egyptian tradition (Eastern), such as the Pachomian rule; the Cappadocian tradition (Eastern), such as Basil's rule; and the North African tradition (Western), such as Augustine's rule. The third was a more direct influence than the second, but the first was the most influential, coming through John Cassian and then the *Rule of the Master* (from an unknown author soon after 500 AD). All had the purpose of regulating the life of monks living in the *coenobium*.

The original rule was considered to be scripture. As monasticism developed, a tradition of interpretation of scripture regarding monasticism developed with a complex of doctrines and observances. The West inherited this tradition from the East and adapted it to fit local circumstances. Thus, a rule writer wrote to apply tradition (which ultimately went back to scripture) to a single community.

Benedict influenced future generations through his rule, not through his activities or personal influence. After the sack of Cassino (577), the fate of Benedict's *Rule* in Italy is a mystery; its future would be in Germanic kingdoms and especially in Gaul.

5. "It's Not All about You, Froshies," *Los Angeles Times*, August 28, 2005, M3.

6. Michael Casey, OCS, *A Guide to Living in the Truth* (Ligouri, MO: Ligouri/Triumph, 2001), 15. Casey does think Benedict's is an "uncharacteristically severe admonition" regarding laughter in 6.8: "there is probably no harm in postponing a campaign to eliminate laughter until some of our more significant vices have been curtailed" (176).

7. See Mark Noll, *The Scandal of the Evangelical Mind* (Grand Rapids: Eerdmans, 1994).

8. Benedictines debate whether they are contemplatives, especially since the word *contemplatio* is not found in the *Rule*. Most would prefer to think that perfection lies not in contemplation and tranquillity (as Cassian prescribed) but in charity, humility, and obedience in community life.

9. See John Calvin, *Institutes of the Christian Relgion*, ed. John T. McNeill, trans. Ford Lewis Battles (Philadelphia: Westminster Press, 1960), 3.6.4.

10. Stanley Grenz, *Theology for the Community of God* (Grand Rapids: Eerdmans, 2000), 15 (citing Donald Dayton).

11. *RB1980: The Rule of St. Benedict in English*, ed. Timothy Fry, OSB (Collegeville, MN: Liturgical Press, 1982).

12. John Getlin, "Time Spent Watching Television Increases," *Los Angeles Times*, September 22, 2006. This statistic is an all-time high, despite competition from iPods, cell phones, DVDs, and satellite radio.

13. Richard John Neuhaus, *Death on a Friday Afternoon* (New York: Basic Books, 2000), 5–6.

14. E.g., see Calvin *Institutes* 1.15.1–4, 2.2.12, 3.3.9–11.

15. Esther deWaal, *Seeking God: The Way of St. Benedict* (Collegeville, MN: Liturgical Press, 1984), 23.

Chapter 3 Learning to Listen

1. The Cistercian Order was founded at Citeaux in 1098 by monks who wanted to establish a more strict and primitive Benedictine practice than what existed at that time. Bernard of Clairvaux became one of its early and rising stars, as the order spread rapidly to nearly every part of Europe and the Latin East. On the eve of the Reformation, there were about seven hundred houses. Cistercians were no exception to the trend of most monastic orders of beginning to move away from the letter of the law to honor its spirit instead, and, as is typical of many orders, in time a more strict group of Cistercians attempted to restore the vision of their founders. These were located in France, including at La Trappe; hence the name Trappists is often associated with Cistercians, though technically they are now designated the Cistercians of the Strict Observance (OCSO) or Reformed Cistercians (OCR). Many people today are familiar with the writings of Thomas Merton, a Cistercian who was associated with the Abbey of Gethsemane in Kentucky. An interesting way to get an idea of Cistercian monasticism is to read *Voices of Silence: Lives of Trappists Today* by Frank Bianco (New York: Anchor, 1991).

2. Columba Stewart, *Prayer and Community: The Benedictine Tradition* (Maryknoll, NY: Orbis, 1998), 51.

3. Anthony Bloom, *Beginning to Pray* (Ramsey, NJ: Paulist, 1970), 68.

4. Casey, *Guide to Living*, 261.

5. This is something like H. Richard Niebuhr's primary point in *The Responsible Self* (Louisville: Westminster John Knox, 1999), 126: "God is acting in all actions upon you. So respond to all actions upon you as to respond to his action."

6. Bloom, *Beginning to Pray*, 45–46.

7. Casey, *Guide to Living*, 174.

8. Ibid., 165.

Chapter 4 Poverty: Sharing the Goods

1. Bloom, *Beginning to Pray*, pp. 41–42.

2. deWaal, *Seeking God*, page 102.

3. Richard Foster, *Freedom of Simplicity*, reprint ed. (San Francisco: Harper, 1998), 110–11.

4. See *RB* 4.44–49 and 7.11.

5. Columba Stewart, *Prayer and Community: The Benedictine Tradition* (Maryknoll, NY: Orbis, 1998), 88.

6. Casey, *Guide to Living*, 123.

Chapter 5 Obedience: Objectifying Providence

1. Columba Stewart makes the case for chastity (which requires God's grace) over against mere abstinence (which depends on willpower) as he develops this central motif in the writings of John Cassian, a fifth-century contemporary of Augustine whose spiritual theology underlies Benedictine spirituality. See *Cassian the Monk* (Oxford: Oxford University Press, 1998), chap. 4. Apparently willpower is not enough. In *The Scandal of the Evangelical Conscience* (Grand Rapids: Baker, 2005), Ronald Sider cites research from Columbia and Yale Universities that found 88 percent of teens who took the "True Love Waits" pledge reported having sexual intercourse before marriage.

2. Thomas Merton, *The Seven Storey Mountain* (New York: Harcourt, Brace, 1948), 372.

3. Dietrich Bonhoeffer, *Life Together*, trans. with an introduction by John W. Doberstein (San Francisco: Harper and Row, 1954), 26–30. Compare this section to *RB* 5.12: "They no longer live by their own judgment, giving in to their whims and appetites; rather they walk according to another's decisions and directions, choosing to live in monasteries and to have an abbot over them." When the monastic enters the monastery, he or she sets out not to change the community but to be transformed by community life—much as one should not enter a marriage to change the spouse but for both to be transformed by having entered into a covenant relationship.

4. Casey, *Guide to Living*, 89.

5. Stewart, *Prayer and Community*, 54–55.

6. Ibid., 65.

7. Brian C. Taylor, *Spirituality for Everyday Living: An Adaptation of the Rule of St. Benedict* (Collegeville, MN: Liturgical Press, 1989), 26.

8. Ibid., 27–28.

9. Joan Chittister, OSB, *Wisdom Distilled from the Daily: Living the Rule of St. Benedict Today* (New York: Harper and Row, 1990), 139.

Chapter 6 Humility: Letting Go of the Mask

1. Casey, *Guide to Living*.

2. See Columba Stewart, "The Desert Fathers on Radical Honesty about the Self," *Sobernost* 12 (1990): 25–39, 131–56; reprinted in *Vox Benedictina* 8 (1991): 7–53.

3. Casey, *Guide to Living*, 26.

4. Ibid., 18–21. The first may seem to go without saying, but Casey reminds us that those who forget they are not gods often cannot forgive themselves for being human.

5. See Joan Chittister, *The Rule of Benedict* (New York: Crossroad, 1992), 70.

6. Casey, *Guide to Living*, 66; also see 42–43.

7. Stewart suggests that the chapter on humility recapitulates the former two; humility is inseparable from obedience and restraint of speech (*Prayer and Community*, 56).

8. Ibid., 57.

9. Donald Miller, *Blue like Jazz* (Nashville: Thomas Nelson, 2003), 20–22.
10. Stewart, *Prayer and Community*, 68.
11. Casey, *Guide to Living*, 150.
12. Ibid.
13. See ibid., 82.
14. See Calvin *Institutes* 3.3.9: "Therefore, in a word, I interpret repentance as regeneration [one of Calvin's synonyms for sanctification], whose sole end is to restore in us the image of God that had been disfigured and all but obliterated through Adam's transgression."
15. See Casey, *Guide to Living*, 10–11.
16. Stewart, *Prayer and Community*, 68.

Chapter 7 Hospitality: The Guest as Christ

1. The early church's celebration of Communion was connected with a meal—the *apage* meal or love feast (hence Paul's admonitions in 1 Corinthians 11 about not demanding a place in the front of the dinner line). Essentially, the Blue Cloud Abbey monks were replicating this on Thursday evenings. The students and I took the idea back to the college and, for a time, invited all who wanted to join us to eat together on Friday evenings in a special room of the dining hall, after which we transitioned into a Communion service.
2. While it might be possible to justify the battle for Cassino in order to defeat the Germans in Italy in World War II, it is highly debatable whether the destruction of the monastery was necessary. An Italian from Cassino said it was the equivalent of Italians' bombing Westminster Abbey. The Germans had promised the Vatican that their troops would not occupy the abbey buildings, and it seems they kept their promise (though they were certainly stationed all around it). While none of the U.S. ground commanders thought that bombing the monastery was warranted, British General Sir Harold Alexander admitted it was done mainly for the effect it would have on the morale of the attacking Allied forces. The result was that the building was entirely demolished except for the lone gate. The irony is that General Frido von Senger, the German commander in charge of the Axis resistance at Cassino, was a Benedictine oblate, and two German soldiers met with the abbot the day before the bombing to discuss the imminent danger of destruction and possible evacuation, all concluding that surely the Allies would never carry out such a threat. The last foreigner to tour the monastery was German Lieutenant Daiber, who requested from the abbot a tour after their meeting. Within hours, on February 15, 1944, the monastery was rubble. See Matthew Parker, *Monte Cassino: The Hardest-Fought Battle of World War II* (New York: Anchor, 2004), 149–83. Also see Tvedten, *How to Be a Monastic*, 70.
3. Carl E. Braaten and Robert W. Jenson, *The Two Cities of God: The Church's Responsibility for the Earthly City* (Grand Rapids: Eerdmans, 1997), back cover.
4. John L'Heureux, *One Eye and a Measuring Rod* (New York: Macmillan, 1968).

Chapter 8 Stability: Staying Put to Get Somewhere

1. See Rodney Clapp, *Families at the Crossroads* (Downers Grove, IL: Inter-Varsity Press, 1993), chap. 4, for the idea that the Christian should consider the church as her "first family," even above her nuclear family.

2. Benet Tvedten's book *The View from a Monastery* captures this sentiment in stories with humor and poignancy. See the list of suggested readings.

3. Thomas Kelly uses this phrase to characterize those whose lives are so harried because they say yes to everything. He reminds us that we can't die on every cross. In the tradition of Friends rather than Benedictines, Kelly's book is insightful and edifying. See *A Testament of Devotion*, with a biographical memoir by Douglas V. Steere (New York: Harper and Row, 1941), 114.

4. Henri Nouwen, *The Genesee Diary* (New York: Doubleday, 1981), 77.

5. Robert Louis Wilken, *The Spirit of Early Christian Thought: Seeking the Face of God* (New Haven: Yale University Press, 2003), 78.

6. Casey, *Guide to Living*, 207n2.

7. Rowan Williams, *Christian Spirituality: A Theological History from the New Testament to Luther and St. John of the Cross* (Atlanta: John Knox, 1979), 105.

8. Ibid., 94–95.

9. Casey, *Guide to Living*, 130.

10. John Henry Newman, *An Essay on the Development of Christian Doctrine*, chap. 1, sec. 1.

Chapter 9 Balance: God in Everything

1. Stewart, *Prayer and Community*, 118.

2. Bonhoeffer, *Life Together*, 69–70.

3. Some of what is said here is to be attributed to various remarks made by Terrence Kardong, Irene Nowell, and Shawn Caruth at the biennial convention of the American Benedictine Academy at St. Benedict's Monastery (St. Joseph, MN) on August 12–14, 2004. Shawn Caruth's remarks are published in vol. 57, no. 2 (June 2006), of *The American Benedictine Review*.

Chapter 10 To Change the World!

1. Justin McCann, *Saint Benedict* (New York: Sheed and Ward, 1937), 20.

2. Stewart, *Prayer and Community*, 68.

3. See Marva Dawn, *Is It a Lost Cause? Having God's Heart for the Church's Children* (Grand Rapids: Eerdmans, 1997), 48–49, for the notion of the church as an "alternative and parallel" culture.

4. Columba Stewart, OSB, a professor at St. John's University in Collegeville, Minnesota (and member of the St. John's monastic community), first called my attention to the eschatological awareness that is rife in the writings of John Cassian and Gregory the Great, during a lecture at the 1996 ABA Convention. Jacques Ellul, the French sociologist and theologian, put it well when he insisted that we Christians are to call the future into the present as an explosive force. We are to help create history by inflecting it toward God's future. In the process, in good monastic style, we can call the "worldly world" to judgment and conversion by

a reality that is not fully existent but is modeled by those who live out Benedict's ideal *now*; see his *The Presence of the Kingdom*, 2nd ed. (Colorado Springs: Helmers and Howard, 1989), 38.

5. See Lesslie Newbigin, *The Gospel in a Pluralist Society* (Grand Rapids: Eerdmans, 1989), chap. 18, where Newbigin uses this phrase to refer to the church congregation.

6. Lesslie Newbigin, *Foolishness to the Greeks* (Grand Rapids: Eerdmans, 1986), 64.

7. Ellul, *Presence of the Kingdom*, 25.

8. C. René Padilla, *Mission between the Times: Essays on the Kingdom* (Grand Rapids: Eerdmans, 1985), 55.

9. Stanley Hauerwas and William H. Willimon, *Resident Aliens: Life in the Christian Colony* (Nashville: Abingdon, 1989), 72.

10. Alisdair MacIntyre, *After Virtue* (Notre Dame, IN: Notre Dame University Press, 1984), 263.

A Historical Afterword: Why the Protestant Reformers Opposed Monasticism

1. John Cassian, *The Conferences*, translated and annotated by Boniface Ramsey, OP (New York: Paulist, 1997), 474.

2. Owen Chadwick, *John Cassian: A Study in Primitive Monasticism* (Cambridge: Cambridge University Press, 1950).

3. Stewart, *Cassian the Monk*.

4. Ibid., 78.

5. If you want to read Cassian's own words about these ideas, look at *Conference* 13, such as passages 9.5, 14.9, and 16.1.

6. Casey, *Guide to Living*, 56–57.

7. See David Steinmetz, *Calvin in Context* (New York: Oxford University Press, 1995), 188–92.

8. Besides secondary sources, criticisms can be read in Zwingli's *Commentary on True and False Religion* (especially sec. 22), Calvin's *Institutes* (especially 4.13), and several of Luther's treatises (such as "An Appeal to the Ruling Class," "On Monastic Vows," and "An Answer to Several Questions on Monastic Vows").

9. Steinmetz, *Calvin in Context*, 194.

10. Ulrich Zwingli, *Commentary on True and False Religion*, ed. Samuel Macauley Jackson and Clarence Nevin Heller (Durham, NC: Labyrinth, 1981), 264. It's interesting that in a very different sense and for very different reasons, dispensationalists have also exempted Christians from the demands of the Sermon on the Mount.

11. Martin Luther, "The Judgment of Martin Luther on Monastic Vows," in *Luther's Works*, vol. 44, *The Christian in Society,* translated by James Atkinson (St. Louis: Concordia Publishing House, 1955–), 288.

12. Ibid., 291.

13. Ibid., 285.

14. Ibid., 295.

15. Ibid., 280.

16. Ibid., 282, 326, 376–77.
17. Ibid., 391.
18. Calvin *Institutes* 4.13.3.
19. Zwingli, *Commentary*, 261–62.
20. Calvin *Institutes*, 4.13.3.
21. Luther, "Judgment of Martin Luther," 384.
22. Stewart, *Cassian the Monk*, 71. See chap. 4 of his book for the discussion in this paragraph.
23. Luther, "Judgment of Martin Luther," 252–54, 294–96.
24. Ibid., 304.
25. Calvin *Institutes* 4.13.4.
26. Stenimetz, *Calvin in Context*, 193–94; see Calvin *Institutes* 4.5.8.
27. Calvin *Institutes* 4.13.16; cf. Luther, "Judgment of Martin Luther," 361.
28. Zwingli, *Commentary*, 262.
29. Casey, *Guide to Living*, 7.
30. See Martin Luther, "An Appeal to the Ruling Class" (1520), in *Martin Luther: Selections from His Writings*, ed. and with an introduction by John Dillenberger (Garden City, NY: Anchor, 1961), 445–47. See Luther, *Works*, 44:253–55, for his praise of monastic founders.
31. Calvin *Institutes* 4.13.9.
32. Ibid. 14.13.8. See Steinmetz, *Calvin in Context*, 193.